NEIGHBOURHOOD
GUIDE TO CYCLING

Naarm — Melbourne

Trent   Kate
Holden & Morgan

Contents

● START ➜ ON THE WAY ⚑ FINISH

Introduction

Multicultural, vibrant Melbourne/Naarm – a city known and celebrated for many things. Not only is this one of the world's greatest sporting cities but it's a UNESCO City of Literature and home to a thriving arts and live-music scene, making it a town for all tastes. From 19th-century grandeur to cutting-edge design; fine dining to cheap and cheerful BYO; bayside beaches to rivers and wetlands; cool inner-city culture to rural relaxed fringes – its variation covers the full gamut. But well before it was called Melbourne, this was an area known as Naarm: the First Nations name that's being used again these days to acknowledge the Traditional Owners of these lands. This is where the Woiwurrung and Boonwurrung Peoples of the Kulin Nation have resided for at least 40,000 years and whose ancient culture – past and present – remains an integral part of the city's fabric.

If you think you know Melbourne pretty well, wait until you get on a bike. As you cycle its trails to discover First Nations history as well as parklands, creeks and wetlands, in between inner-city backstreets and bush-filled outer suburbs that have inspired generations of famous artists, writers and musicians, it casts a whole new light on the city. Melbourne's appeal perhaps lies more in its experiential charms than the sights itself, and this is precisely what makes it such a great place to explore by bike.

All you need to do is look at the astronomical rise in bikes sales to see that Melbourne has truly embarked on a new era of cycling. The past few years have seen a staggering increase of 400 per cent in bicycle sales, and demand has been so great that, in some cases, there's a wait of months (if not years) on certain models. Though these figures are driven by the advent of Covid and Melbourne's lockdowns, even well before the pandemic it was a fast-rising trend. Locals are not only seeking a healthier lifestyle, but a greener, cheaper and more time-effective alternative to the city's traffic-clogged roads and unreliable public transport system.

The past decade or so has seen Melbourne quietly establish itself as one of the world's most bike-friendly cities. Taking you off busy roads, its vast and varied network of dedicated bike routes are so intertwined that riding here is a bit like a Choose Your Own Adventure. Rail trails, creek trails, coastal trails, highway trails and inner-city trails: your options are limitless as you chop and change at a whim, going everywhere from the city into remnant bushland, outer-city beaches and lesser-visited suburbs, all within an easy day's ride.

And while Melbourne may have some way to go in matching the cycling capital of the world, Amsterdam, if the amount of pop-up shared bike lanes appearing seemingly overnight is anything to go by, it's well on track. So, as we find ourselves now in what is unquestionably a golden age of cycling, never has there been a better time to get on two wheels and get better acquainted with Marvellous Melbourne.

Trent Holden and Kate Morgan

We would like to acknowledge the Wathaurong People, Traditional Custodians of the land on which we live and work. We would also like to acknowledge the Wurundjeri People, the Traditional Custodians of the land on which this book is set. We pay our respects to their Elders past and present.

Which Bike is Right for You?

When it comes to choosing a bike, there are many factors you'll need to consider: your budget; the size of the bike you need; and how you're going to use it (just jumping on and pedalling off is not as simple as it sounds). Will you be cycling as a way to commute to and from work? Are you planning on spending your weekends thrashing around on dusty, rugged mountain-bike trails or do you simply just want to cruise along a beachside boardwalk looking cool and not breaking a sweat? Do you need storage for a backpack, laptop bag or a place to pop your fresh produce after a visit to the local market? Are you here to burn kilojoules or are you happy for an e-bike to do all the legwork?

Once you have the answers to these questions, you'll have more of an idea when it comes to choosing your bike. There is a huge range of bikes out there these days, so here's a quick rundown on the main types you'll come across.

MOUNTAIN BIKE

Mountain bikes or MTBs are a very popular style of bicycle and one best suited for riders who want a bit of grit and gravel on their ride. They usually have suspension, sturdy brakes and thick tyres to handle off-road trails and rough surfaces. But even if you don't plan on tackling steep hills and muddy paths, a mountain bike is still a good choice as they are versatile and can also be used on paved terrain and bike paths. They are on the heavier side, though, so keep that in mind if you have to tackle stairs at home or if you'll be lugging it onto bike racks or elsewhere, and you won't build up the same kind of pace you can on a road bike.

ROAD BIKE

No surprises as to where you might usually ride this style of bike – sealed roads and paved trails. Generally made of lightweight materials, with thinner tyres and drop-down handlebars, road bikes are built more for

speed rather than comfort. The design allows riders to assume a more aerodynamic position to reduce wind drag and is great for road racing. They're the type of bike you choose if you feel the need for speed and want to get fit at the same time.

HYBRID

As the name suggests, hybrid bikes are a fusion of the popular features of other bike styles, so you can think of them as the all-rounder style of bike. If you're looking for a road bike or commuting bike that is lightweight and speedy but still has the feel of something a bit sturdier like a mountain bike, hybrids are the choice for you. They usually have slightly wider tyres than a road bike (great for navigating tram tracks). and they favour comfort and features suitable for urban and recreational cycling over being suited to racing or long off-road, rough trails.

E-BIKE

E-bikes (electric bikes) or power-assisted bikes are everywhere these days as people opt for a more sustainable, greener way of commuting without all that pesky, sweaty work! You still need to pedal but the 'assistance' kicks in to give you that extra  helping hand when you need to tackle a hill or your legs are just simply too tired to work too hard. They have motors that are generally powered by removable lithium-ion batteries and most can get up to speeds of 25km/h (the legal maximum limit in Australia). The downsides are that they are expensive, heavy to lug around and you need to ensure they are charged (and have enough battery power to get you home again). There is a huge range of e-bikes from fat-tyred, high-end mountain bikes to retro cruiser–style bikes.

CRUISER/RETRO BIKES

Becoming more and more popular, the cruiser bike is for anyone looking to get from A to B while everyone envies how stylish you look. They're pretty affordable, comfortable

with plush saddles, upright seated position and curved handlebars, and best suited for city and recreational riding on fairly flat terrain. And these good-looking bikes generally come with all the bells (literally) and whistles, such as a cute straw basket, a bag rack, fenders and so on. Single-speed is the norm but they also come in styles that offer a few gears for those slight inclines on your way to the beach or market.

FIXIES

Long the go-to choice for inner-city cyclists, the 'fixie' is arguably the quintessential Melbourne bike. Though single-speed bikes are popular for those wanting to cruise around neighbourhood streets, they're not really conducive to a long day's easy riding on the trails, particularly if there are hills. But if you want a cool, hipster-looking bike to get around the city on mostly flat terrain, check out the range of fixies on offer.

FOLDABLE BIKES

Foldable bikes are a convenient option for riders who want or need to combine public transport with their daily ride. They are designed to fold down so that they don't take up much space and can be easily carried. These are a good option not only for buses especially (which otherwise don't accept bikes), but also for crowded trains, making it the prototype for the modern-day commuter bike. Though used more for urban rides, you can also take them on the paths and there are models for rougher terrain, too.

RECUMBENT BIKES

If you're looking for a different style of ride, then a recumbent bike could be an option. These bikes are designed to have cyclists positioned in a reclined position at the back, rather than sitting upright, to pedal forward with more of a pushing motion while sitting closer to the ground. These are a popular choice with riders with disabilities, those with back injuries or just after a more comfortable and leisurely style bike. Many are three-wheelers, making them easier to balance and navigate in the same mould as a trike, though check to ensure the model is suitable for gravel.

BMX

If you fantasise about thrashing around town, working on your moves at the local skate park or you're after a gang of bike robbers just like Nicole Kidman in *BMX Bandits* then you're in luck: it's not the '80s anymore but the classic BMX is still very much around. These robust bikes can tackle any dirt jump you care to face; they're considered fairly indestructible (tip: great choice for kids), generally affordable, lightweight and very nostalgic for '80s kids. Likewise, low-riders are another option if you want to cruise around town with the high handlebars looking like a bad-ass.

PENNY-FARTHING

We're not gonna lie: the penny-farthing is not the most practical choice of bike, but lo and behold, somehow these antiquated 19th-century bicycles have made somewhat of a comeback. So, if you want to stand out from the crowd and get a good view, you can't go past the penny-farthing. Frenchman Eugène Meyer is considered the creator of the first 'high wheeler' in around 1869.

The penny-farthing name comes from the large and small wheels of the bicycle resembling the penny and farthing (quarter-penny) coins. Though the bicycles were out of production by 1890, you can still find enthusiasts today who will make you a custom penny-farthing. Just don't hit a pebble as you're at risk of a header (taking a tumble headfirst over the handlebars!).

Cycle Smart and Stay Safe

We know you're raring to get going with your ride but, before you pedal off, it's important to familiarise yourself with some safety tips, cyclists' road rules and general etiquette. Even if you plan on sticking to the dedicated bike paths, there are still regulations that you'll need to be on top of.

CHECK EQUIPMENT BEFORE RIDING

First things first. Don't pop yourself in the riding seat until you've checked the operation of your brakes, gears, lights and bell.

KEEP YOUR NOGGIN SAFE

Make sure your have an approved and well-fitting helmet. It's not necessary to fork out for the latest aerodynamic model, but it should fit firmly (not wobble around loosely on your head) and comfortably (where the strap is not choking you to death).

TRAM TRACKS TRAP

A very Melbourne problem facing bike riders is the scourge of getting your wheel wedged in tram tracks. Everyone knows someone who at some point has come off his or her bike due to this common

problem. To avoid a potentially nasty injury (let alone embarrassment), never turn directly onto the tracks and instead cross at a wide angle or directly over them. And if cars are blocking the bike lane, it may be best to come to a stop rather than hastily turning to fall into the tram tracks.

NO HOONS ALLOWED

Always stick to a safe and sensible speed limit, especially if you're riding an electric bike. On certain roads and bike paths there might be limits, particularly heavily pedestrianised areas such as Southbank (where it's 10km/h), so keep an eye out for signs.

OBEY THE TRAFFIC RULES

Just because you're on two wheels instead of four doesn't mean you are free to do what you like. You must still stop at red lights and stop signs, and be sure to give way to pedestrians at a crossing and so forth. Take note: there is no riding on footpaths unless you are under 13 years old or a supervisor riding with a child under the age of 13.

When cycling on the road and stopping at traffic lights, you might come across a bike box with a bike symbol inside it. This indicates that you must stop inside the box. It provides a safer place to stay clear of the traffic and gives you a head start on the cars when the lights change.

While there are no shortage of places to stop off for a cheeky mid-ride drink... or two, or three, keep in mind that yes, it's illegal to cycle when drunk or drug affected, so stay under the limit. Though with that said, police are not allowed to breathalyse cyclists unless they break the law.

PARKING

If you want to make a pit stop during your ride, make sure you bring a bike lock with you to park your bike safely while you head off exploring, eating, whatever. Bike theft is rife, so avoid leaving your bike unlocked even just to quickly head into a shop, and be sure to lock it tight to an immovable object and one you can't lift it over! In some spots there'll be dedicated bike racks, but it's also fine to park somewhere on the footpath or locked to a pole or whatever fixture you can find, as long as it's not in a clearly signed 'No Parking' area, not private property (i.e. don't go locking your bike to someone's front gate) and not in the way of pedestrians, other cyclists or cars.

OBEY THE BIKE PATH RULES
Some of the bike trails in this book take you on shared bike–pedestrian paths. They are usually clearly marked with a bike or pedestrian symbol to tell you what lane to be in. If you need to overtake another cyclist or pedestrian, be sure to give a polite ding on your bell to let everyone know you're 'passing'. Always watch out for pedestrians crossing the bike path too; sometimes they don't realise they are walking straight from their parked car across a bike path to get the beach, for example. Slow down and give them a ding if need be.

MAKE YOURSELF VISIBLE
Bikes don't have indicators like cars do, so consider your arms and hands your indicators. Always use hand signals to let drivers know what you're intending to do. If you're making a right turn, stick your right arm out with enough time to indicate before your turn. If you're making a left

turn, obviously it's your left arm. Keep a keen eye out for car doors opening when riding past parked cars and try to keep a safe distance from them, but also making sure you're a safe distance from moving traffic. Defensive cycling is always the best approach in that anticipating the many dangers can help you avoid them.

If riding at night, it's crucial you wear reflective gear (a vest, a reflective light sticker on your helmet) and have working lights on the front of our bike (in the centre of your handlebars) and a rear light above the rear tyre.

TRANSPORTING YOUR BIKE

You can take your bike on a Melbourne metro and V/Line trains, but just don't board at the first door of the front carriage, as this is for wheelchair users and mobility scooters. Don't park your bike right in front of the door or the aisle, for obvious reasons. Currently, only a few bus routes have bike racks installed on the front of the buses (there are plans for more to be added in future), and trams are a no-go unless you have a folding bike.

USEFUL RESOURCES

Head to these handy websites to find out more information on safe cycling, road rules and getting your bike around on public transport.

Bicycle Network:

🌐 `bicyclenetwork.com.au`

VicRoads:

🌐 `vicroads.vic.gov.au/traffic-and-road-use/cycling`

Public Transport Victoria:

🌐 `ptv.vic.gov.au/more/travelling-on-the-network/`
`bikes-on-public-transport`

Zen and the Art of Bicycle Maintenance

BASIC DIY BIKE REPAIR

With all the joys of cycling comes the reality that things don't always go to plan. Punctures, flat tyres, loose chains – you'd be unlucky, but these things do happen from time to time. And while there's usually a fellow cyclist passing to lend a hand, it's wise to learn some of the basic DIY skills so these maintenance issues won't mean an end to your day out pedalling around.

First thing is to get organised with a bike repair toolkit, which should at least include the following:

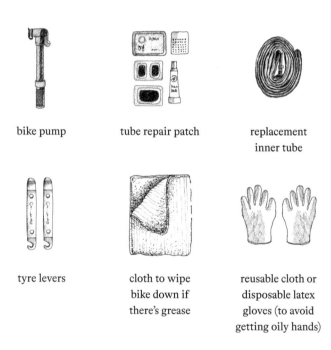

bike pump

tube repair patch

replacement inner tube

tyre levers

cloth to wipe bike down if there's grease

reusable cloth or disposable latex gloves (to avoid getting oily hands)

GENERAL BIKE MAINTENANCE

To keep your bike in tip-top shape, it's important to follow a few maintenance tips. Store your bike out of the weather to avoid issues of rusting, and give the moving parts an occasional oil. If you get any oil or grease on your bike, wipe it down with a cloth as soon as you can, and clean off any dirt and mud build-up with a soapy wash and hose down, then dry off with an old towel or rag.

HOW TO PUMP UP YOUR TYRES

Before you head off on a bike ride it's a good idea to check the air in your tyres. If they are under-inflated, you'll find the bike's performance decreases and you need to put in more effort to ride . . . and that's the last thing you want for a long day ahead of you.

There are a few ways to pump up the tyres, but the quickest and easiest way is to get yourself a bike pump (you can also take your bike to a bike repair store or service station, while many trails have bike pumps along the route). Before pumping up the tyres it's a good idea to know what pressure your particular bike tyres should be (see if it's labelled on the tyres, check your bike product manual or get in touch with your local bike store). Pressure is measured in kPa (kilopascals) – which have replaced the still-found measure of pounds per square inch (psi). But as a general rule, use the following:

- thick tyres for mountain bikes and similar, 200–340 kPa or 30–50 psi

- medium tyres for hybrids, 340–480 kPa or 50–70 psi

- narrow tyres for road bikes, 550–900 kPa or 80–130 psi

- kids' bikes, 140–270 kPa or 20–40 psi.

Most bike tyres commonly have what's called a Schrader valve, the same as those found on car tyres. Unscrew the valve cap and connect the pump head onto the valve. Don't worry if you hear air escaping from the tyre at first; that'll take care of itself once you start pumping up the tyre. When the tyre is at the desired pressure (or just when it feels firm enough), disconnect the pump and screw the valve cap back on. Don't over-inflate, or the tube may burst. Then away you go!

HOW TO FIX A TYRE PUNCTURE

While uncommon, tyre punctures do happen on occasion and are something you should be prepared for. Sooner or later you come across a sharp rock or shard of broken glass and you're out of action. Under-inflated tyres and old tyres that need replacing can also be a contributing factor. But don't let a little puncture ruin your ride; learn how to DIY repair your way out of it.

Small punctures

If an object has caused the puncture, a tyre patch can be a quick way to fix it up. Pop some in your toolkit for emergency repairs. Locate the puncture site, pull out the offending object and pop on the patch. Pump up the tyre in case of any lost air and be on your way.

Big punctures

If you don't have any patches or the puncture is quite bad/big, you'll need to replace the tyre's inner tube. It sounds complicated but you just need to follow a few simple steps.

1   Remove the wheel with the puncture and completely deflate the tyre by depressing the tyre valve.

2   Grab your tyre levers from your kit and slide them between the tyre and the rim of the wheel then lever the tyre loose.

3   Remove the deflated tube.

4   Check the sidewalls of the tyre for any object
     or cuts.

5   Inflate your replacement inner tube just enough to hold shape,
     then work it into the tyre with your thumbs.

6   Once it's in the tyre, inflate it fully, place the wheel back on,
     and you're done!

HOW TO FIX A DROPPED CHAIN

One of the most annoying things that can go wrong mid-ride, perhaps a
close second to a puncture, is a chain that decides to come loose. Known as
a dropped chain, it can all be a bit fiddly and messy to get back on but with
a bit of know-how and patience, you can have it back in place – and be out
of an excuse to cut the ride short to head home – before you know it.

1   Pop your latex gloves on to avoid making a
     mess. Flip your bike upside down so that the
     handlebars are resting on the ground and the
     tyres are in the air where it's easier to get at
     the chain. There are a few points where the
     chain can come loose but often it's from the
     small gear on the rear tyre axle.

2   Loosen the rear tyre levers or bolts, depending
     on the type of bike.

3   Pull the wheel back, away from the
     handlebars, so that the chain is taut and place
     the chain back around the small gear, all while
     ensuring the wheel is kept straight.

4   Once you have the chain back on the gear, slide
     the wheel back in place and tighten the lever
     or bolts to secure.

BIKE REPAIRS WITH LOVE

Whether you're a daily commuter, a weekend rider or just your hands-on-DIY-kinda type, then consider signing up for a crash course in bike repair with one of the following not-for-profit organisations. As well as workshops, services and repairs, all provide a wonderful training ground for volunteers (from newbies up) where you'll learn to tinker with donated second-hand bikes under the supervision of experienced mechanics. The bikes are refurbed and then sold on to the local community. All are volunteer-based, community-driven, environmentally conscious and diversity-minded.

Back2Bikes (back2bikes.com.au) Established in 2012, this not-for-profit is based in Port Melbourne and run by a team of volunteers who repair and refurb bikes as well as run workshops on bicycle maintenance.

Community Bike Hub (communitybikehub.com.au) This social enterprise in Footscray offers bike servicing, sells refurbed bikes and donates bikes to asylum seekers. They also run workshops and school holiday programs. They're in Torquay, too.

Good Cycles (goodcycles.org.au) Another not-for-profit is this bike shop empowering members of the community through its mechanic trainee programs. Based in the Docklands and CBD as well as Geelong.

The Bike Shed (thebikeshed.org.au) Set up at CERES in East Brunswick, this community organisation accepts volunteers; and is another good spot to pick up a bike.

Hiring a Bike and Touring the Town

Just getting into the idea of cycling and wanting to test the waters before forking out for a new bike? Or perhaps you've finally dusted off your 20-year-old bike from the garage and it's more worse for wear than you remember? Or is it time to go electric, but you're not sure if you'll like it? Well that's where a bike rental comes in handy. Before you splash out the cash for a sparkling new bike, it's not a bad idea to hire one first to see if you think you have what it takes to be the next Cadel Evans, or just to make sure cycling is something you actually enjoy and the reality of helmet hair and a tender bum doesn't put you right off.

There are plenty of great bike hire shops spread around the city offering road bikes, mountain bikes, e-bikes, hybrids, kids' bikes and tandem for those luvvy-duvvy romantics out there. And if you want to get a feel for riding in a guided group situation before you strike out on your own, you can join any numbers of tours around town. Here are a few of our favourites bike hire spots.

ST KILDA CYCLES
stkildacycles.com.au
5 Vale St, St Kilda
9534 3074

This spacious bike shop, tucked off Barkly St in St Kilda, is a great pick for anyone looking to hire some wheels for a short cruise along the Esplanade or a day riding out to **Half Moon Bay** (p40) for some fish'n' chips and a dip in the bay. Standard bikes only ($40 per day) – no e-bikes available at the time of writing – but these will do the job on the flat terrain around St Kilda and the ride to Half Moon Bay. St Kilda Cycles do rent out some smaller mountain bikes for kids but check in advance. If you're in the market for a bike, there is a large range on offer here, along with all your accessory needs such as helmets, locks, bike racks, bells and lights. There is a 'bike mechanic' on duty should you need a puncture repair and you're 'not keen to give it a go yourself (p12).

VELO CYCLES

velocycles.com.au

815 Nicholson St, Carlton North

9381 0088

Situated just off the **Capital City Trail** (p28) on the corner of Park and Nicholson streets in Carlton North, Velo Cycles is a one-stop shop for all your bike hire, service and purchase needs. It offers standard bikes at $40 a day, e-bikes are $100 for the day or, if you plan on hopping on and off public transport, then a cool folding Brompton bike is the perfect choice ($50). And if after a day of riding around you find you simply can't part with your bike, Velo will deduct the rental cost from the purchase price of the bike.

BLUE TONGUE BIKES

bluetonguebikes.com.au

20 Rebecca Walk, Batman Park, Melbourne

0490 553 673

Conveniently located, friendly service, a range of bikes to rent and plenty of expertise – Blue Tongue ticks all your cycling needs. You'll find it in Batman Park in the city centre near the Yarra's edge, a short walk from SEA LIFE Aquarium. Bike hire starts at $25 for two hours, or $35 for all day (e-bikes start at $40), and will have you cruising around in style on chic, Dutch-brand Lekker bikes. Blue Tongue also offers a number of great bike tours, including their Bike 'n' Brews ride around the craft beer breweries of Melbourne's hipster inner north. And if you have your own wheels but they need a bit of lovin', you can get all your bike servicing and repairs taken care of here, too (basic service $60).

MELBOURNE BY BIKE

melbournebybike.com

Federation Square, Swanston St, Melbourne

0417 339 203

Established back in 1976, this is one of Melbourne's oldest bike rentals and is best known for its well-curated city tours that depart from Federation Square daily at 10am.

LIME BIKES

You've probably seen one or two of these garish flame-orange/red Lime bikes parked inappropriately in the middle of a street, abandoned in a parking lot or shoved in some bushes on the side of cycling trail. Lime is a dockless e-bike-share scheme  (which also introduced e-scooters in early 2022) that operates in the City of Melbourne, the City of Port Phillip and the City of Yarra local government areas.

To borrow one, first, you'll need to download the Lime bike app (li.me) or you can rent them via the Uber app, too. You'll see a map that tells you the location sites of e-bikes. Each bike has a QR code on it. Scan the code via the app and enter the number on the wheel hub to unlock. You'll get instructions on using the bike, too. And then you're all set! When you're done, you need to return the bike to the nearest Lime bike site (again, check the map: don't be one of those people who abandon them all over town).

As for helmets, they come with the bike, and then you can loop them through the cable when you lock it up once you're finished with the bike.

There is a $1 activation fee to unlock the bikes, then it's 45c per minute. You can buy a 24-hour pass for $17. These bikes are by far the cheapest option, so what are they like to ride? If you're sticking to the paved bike paths, they're a reliable choice, though some cyclists find them a little lumbering and uncomfortable. They're best avoided if you plan on cycling largely along gravel trails.

Accessible Cycling

As Melbourne becomes more bike-friendly by the year, it also becomes more accessible for cyclists living with mobility issues. While there's still a long way to go in terms of improving infrastructure, the installation of ramps and lifts in public buildings and train stations across the city has seen it become much easier to navigate in the past five years. And with the rise of custom-made adaptive bikes, trikes, recumbents, tandems and handcycles, never has there been a better time for cyclists with mobility issues to get pedalling along all those new bike lanes and dedicated trails. Plus, cycling is an ideal way to feel a greater sense of independence and accessibility, and there's a proven link between the benefits of outdoor exercise and wellbeing.

Broadly speaking, cyclists with mobility issues can expect to face the same challenges as wheelchair and mobility aid users. But some of the larger bikes (namely recumbent and cargo bikes) can be tougher to squeeze through tighter spaces, such as railway pedestrian crossings or weaving through some the chicanes found on the rural bike trails. While some adaptive bikes can be more difficult to fit inside cars, a lot are designed to be disassembled (i.e. stabilising wheels can be removed) making them easier to transport.

HOW TO GET STARTED

Many bicycle stores can help out with customising new bikes for those with specific needs, including elderly cyclists, by making adjustments for optimal fitting and dexterity. For something more individualised, get in touch with the not-for-profit **Freedom Wheels** (`freedomwheels.org.au`), a wonderful organisation specialising in bikes and services for riders living with disabilities. You can book in a time each Wednesday and Thursday at their Abbotsford location to trial bikes, obligation-free. If all goes well, the bike will then be designed and adjusted to your needs in what is a collaborative process. It's run by a workforce comprising largely volunteers or retired mechanics and engineers who will set about building the bike. They offer a range of styles and designs for both kids and adults.

If you're not in a position to ride yourself, then get in touch with **Cycling Without Age** (`cyclingwithoutage.org.au`), a worldwide not-for-profit organisation that takes those with a lack of mobility (of all ages) for a scenic ride around Melbourne on modified cargo-cycle trishaws.

Local Chit-chat with Stuart Tripp

Stuart Tripp is a father, husband and Paralympic champion cyclist who has represented Australia at the London (2012), Rio (2016) and Tokyo (2021) Games. He's also written an autobiography *Travelling Hopefully* and has another book in the works. Read more at `paralympic.org.au/athlete/stu-tripp`

You're a three-time Paralympian and silver medallist. It must've been an honour to represent Australia at the highest level?

Is it an honour to represent your country? Yes it is. More important than the honour is the people who get you there. The coaches, sports scientists, the physios, the dietician, the psychologist, the doctor, the administrators ... the list is long.

My role is simple: ride the bike. Which I ride for my mental health – and representing your country is the cream on the cake. The real accolades go to the people who enable me to do that.

But I achieved that honour by accident, a real car accident (in 1994). I wasn't a kid who dreamed of becoming an athlete – I was never that good at sport – but I always turned up. I would often get the best clubman's award. I had no desire, no interest or ambition to be an athlete. It wasn't until five years after my accident, while going through a nervous breakdown, that a psychologist suggested that I do some exercises to help with my mental health. This was in 2000, well before the general public at large recognised that exercise was great for your mental health.

To be honest, if that man had suggested you crawl over broken glass for 5 metres, I would have been the first person breaking bottles, I was in such a state of distress. I started by swimming, then handcycling, then state champion, then national champion, then my first World Championships event, World Cups. It took me eight years of failing before I won an international event.

And you competed in the New York Marathon too?

Yes I did. Through a fortuitous series of chance meetings I met Jack, a personal trainer. At the time, I was living in Traralgon with my parents, but I explained to Jack that I wanted to move back to Melbourne, and he immediately said he had the place for me. I asked was it ground floor? He affirmed. Was it wheelchair accessible? He affirmed. When could I move in? Straight away. Boom. I moved into an apartment in Elwood the next month, and spent ten years there, the longest time I've been in one place, except for my childhood home. Elwood was very transformative for me. In late 2003, I got my first handcycle and fell deeply in love with the concept. One day in October 2003, I was riding around Albert Park Lake, on the running track, because at that stage I wasn't confident or comfortable riding on roads, and I ran into Jack. I was that excited about the bike and being outdoors and the freedom it provided – I was pumped. Jack asked me, what was my goal? And without thinking I responded: to do the New York marathon. Where did that come from?

At the time I weighed 115 kilograms – the rated weight for the handcycle was 110 kilograms; I smoked two packs of soft-pack Stuyvesants a day; I ate pretty poorly; I drank too much and I was self-medicating.

An old schoolmate was running the New York marathon in 2003, a guy who I played under-10s football against right through to under-16 and then we played as teammates in the under-18 Traralgon team. So I did some research on the New York marathon, and found out they accepted handcycle entries.

Three months later, I get a call out of the blue from Jack, 'yeah mate, how you going?', 'good mate, I've just paid the deposit on your entry to the New York Marathon for 2004, you up for it?'

I was blown away. Anyway, that was the start of the New York marathon story. Yes, I did it; yep, completed it – a whole story in itself – and had a great time.

And what are some of your favourite rides in Melbourne?

Southside I'd pick Beach Rd, where your two options are 'on road' for confident riders, and the bike path for less confident. Northside I'd pick the Kew Boulevard and the dedicated bike path along the Yarra Trails from Kew Boulevard to the Eastern Freeway tunnels.

And as someone who rides a handcycle, what tips do you have for cyclists getting around Melbourne?

First and foremost is feel safe in your own abilities. If it's not safe, it's not enjoyable. Second would be use known cycling routes on cycle paths or road routes, and thirdly, ride like you own the road but accept you're only an addendum and be safe; ride for the conditions and the traffic, be it vehicular or foot.

Cycling with Kids

What better way to enjoy some quality family time together than a good ol'-fashioned bike ride? Taking in everything from shipwrecks, billabongs and wetlands to beaches and a network of river systems, each of Melbourne's trails can be treated like a mini-adventure, exploring new environments that'll have you feeling like a tourist in your own town. Each comes with its own unique flavour, loaded with history and local tales, and not only delivers in the educational stakes but also provides an opportunity for fresh air and exercise – any chance to get the kids off their devices and active outdoors is a win. And once they hear what's on the itinerary – swims in the bay, boat rides, ice-cream, toy shops and even theme parks – it won't take much convincing to get them on their bikes.

Got a couple of young tackers in tow? Don't worry, you don't need to commit to riding the whole trail. Each can be broken-down into bite-size chunks and there's family-friendly highlights at the start. In fact, doing smaller sections is a good way of allowing you to put the focus more on fun than trying to see everything at once and turning it into a tough slog.

WHICH BIKE?

There is a heap of choices for kids' bikes, but your best bet for tackling Melbourne's trails and neighbourhood routes is an entry-level mountain bike. Also known as recreational bikes, these are no-frills models that come with a few gears for uphill sections and have a sturdy design to make them easier for balancing and braking. It's important to get the right size bike, so be sure to go to a reputable bike store with staff who can provide expert advice. Kids' e-bikes are less common, not to mention costly (and they'll outgrow them), so they're not really a great option.

BABY SEATS AND TRAILERS

For younger children who are either not old enough to ride alone or won't have enough puff to go long distances, you can fit your own bike with a kid's chair at the back or front, so they

can hitch a ride with you. A trailer, which is attached to the rear of the bike and pulled along, is another great safe option. It's probably best avoided if you plan on riding a fair bit on gravel paths or steep inclines, or at least make sure you have the right tyres fitted and get a trailer with good suspension. Most trailers have a zip-up covering to shield the kids from adverse weather and are like mini pedicabs, with the added bonus of space for storage (snacks, nappies and so on). You can also get a double trailer if you need to fit a couple of little ones in there. It's not a bad idea to do a test drive with your kids in it to see how it all feels for both the rider and passenger in terms of comfort, balance and space.

ROAD SAFETY

If your kids are too young or lack the confidence to ride on the road, rest assured that children under 13 years are allowed to ride on the footpath – and likewise those accompanying them. But be sure to look out for pedestrians coming in and out of shops, and cars backing out of driveways. If you're still a bit nervous about your kids getting out on trails and neighbourhood routes, then you can consider taking them to a bike school to learn the basic dos and don'ts first.

The traffic schools are usually set up as a miniature grid system of streets, complete with traffic lights, stop signs, roundabouts and other road simulations – even trams and trains – and children will get firsthand knowledge on how to get around in accordance with the road rules in a safe environment. Here are a few places you can try:

- **Essendon Traffic School** (mvcc.vic.gov.au/play/my-experience/essendon-traffic-school)

- **Kew Traffic School** (boroondara.vic.gov.au/recreation-arts/sportsgrounds-and-sports-facilities/kew-traffic-school)

- **Brimbank Bicycle Education Centre** (brimbankbicycleed.com)

- **Camelot Traffic School** (facebook.com/CamelotTSchool)

WHAT TO BRING

Beyond the usual accessories, including helmets, locks, reflectors, bike-repair kit, first-aid kit, sunscreen and insect repellent, there are a few other things you'll want to add to your backpack:

- binoculars for birdwatching; a bird book, too, or an app such as the *Michael Morcombe eGuide to Australian Birds*

- bathers, towel, snorkel, goggles for coastal rides

- Frisbee, footy, ball for parks

- picnic blanket

- water, healthy snacks for energy and some treats for 'motivation'

- the right clothing: make sure kids have short sleeves for when they get too hot from riding, as well as warm jackets, rain gear and jumpers for cooler days or if the weather turns.

TOP TIPS FOR RIDING WITH KIDS

- Kids will get tired out more quickly than you do, so, before you head out, take a look at the map to check what section of a ride best suits you, rather than trying to tackle an entire trail.

- Treats along the ride will go a long way, and the promise of ice-cream 'a bit further ahead' will also add a bit of an incentive to keep pedalling.

- Variety is key, so be sure to build in stops for parks, kicks of the footy, swims, food – and toilets.

- Despite the many tasty temptations along the trail, you don't have to fork out on food along the way: instead come with a packed picnic to enjoy for lunch.

- A checklist for birds is a good way to keep kids motivated, but you can also create your own scavenger hunt for things to tick off, too.

CREATE YOUR OWN BIKE ART

In addition to the routes covered in this book, a further fun idea for families is to map out your own ride using the Strava app (strava.com) to create your own GPS artwork. Google the kinds of designs you can create. Routes can take the shape of anything
you want: from dinosaurs and Darth Vader to word messages and Mona Lisa. But you don't need to be Da Vinci to come up with your own masterpiece; in fact, initially it's best to keep things simple until you get the hang of things. It can take a bit of trial and error, but generally the best way is to draw a rough draft of your picture before printing out the map to then plot it by hand along the streets in the area you want to head off to. Given how closely you'll be engaging with the map on your device, remember: safety always comes first, so be sure to come to a stop before looking at your phone. And don't let it ruin your day if an unexpected detour or network black spot derails your handiwork; you just gotta roll with it. But hopefully when you've finished your ride – ta-da! Your artwork will be logged on your smartphone to keep as a memento of the day's pedalling.

MELBOURNE

BIKE TRAILS

CAPITAL CITY TRAIL

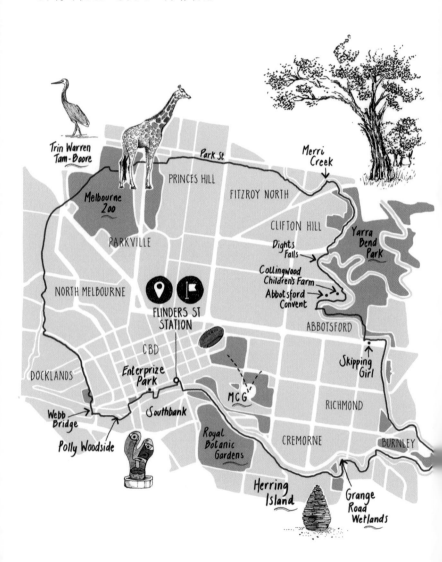

START // FINISH
Flinders Street station

DISTANCE
30km loop

DURATION
3-6 hours

PUBLIC TRANSPORT
All trains lead to Flinders
Street station

CONNECTING RIDES
Gardiners Creek Trail

Main Yarra Trail

**Merri Creek Trail
(p84)**

Moonee Ponds Creek
Trail

Upfield Trail

Featuring Melbourne's landmark attractions, this
showcase ride takes you past the city's most iconic
stops in between character-filled suburbs, idyllic
stretches of bushland and picturesque river bends.

THIS IS IT: Melbourne's flagship ride, a grand parade around the city to give you a glimpse of everything that gave the town its enduring nickname, Marvellous Melbourne. Whether you're a born-and-bred Melburnian or new to the city, this is the one ride you don't want to miss. Skirting the city centre, it traces the course of the beautiful Yarra River/Birrarung and its tributary creeks in what is a highlights reel of pretty much every Melbourne landmark, with some unexpected finds along the way.

🚲 **CYCLING WITH KIDS:** If any bike ride is made for families, it's this one. As it's quite long, we advise divvying it up into a few rides. Enjoy Southbank's buskers and gelato, and stop anywhere from **SEA LIFE Aquarium and Polly Woodside** to **DreamCity** (dreamcity.com.au), before the entertainment possibilities at Docklands, from ice-skating (obrienicehouse.com.au) to boat rides (aquadonut.com) and indoor playgrounds (chipmunksplayland.com.au). **Melbourne Zoo** is a destination in itself. The inner suburbs offer kid-friendly cafes and then bushland on the way to **Dights Falls**, with **Collingwood Children's Farm** ahead. For the last leg, have a look around the open-air gallery at **Herring Island** before finishing up back in the city.

● **WHEN IT COMES TO CULTURAL ICONS**, Melburnians like them weird and wonderful – an ugly digital clock that hasn't told the time in decades, an oddball advertisement for vinegar (of all things) and a 'Birdman rally' that has participants launching themselves into the river in whacky homemade flying machines. So it's only fitting that this ride should begin with an idiosyncratic Melbourne ritual – by 'meeting under the clocks'. It's a time-honoured tradition, and one uttered down through the generations, to meet out front of Flinders Street station. Dating to 1854, the station is Australia's oldest, but its current building, with a beautiful domed, French Renaissance-inspired baroque design – complete with upstairs ballroom – wasn't completed till 1910.

Just under the clocks is another nostalgia-inducing sight for Melburnians, **City Hatters** (`cityhatters.com.au`), which has been fitting Akubras and Stetsons for locals since 1910 from its corner store nook that was the former stationmaster's office.

➔ **FROM HERE**, wheel your bike round to the right to the far end of the station to exit at the Yarra River, where you'll find Melbourne's longest bar, the riverfront **Arbory** (`arbory.com.au`) that stretches 120m along the station. This was the platform from the old Sandridge Line that connected Port Melbourne to the city up until 1987, and you'll follow it further ahead to pedal over the 19th-century **Sandridge Bridge**, where Melbourne's first wave of postwar immigrants arrived from Station Pier. Today it's a footbridge over the Yarra, best known for the **Travellers**, a series of metal sculptures that celebrates the city's multicultural fabric. Crossing the bridge will land you in **Southbank**, the city's riverside dining precinct fronted by a shared pedestrian–cyclist promenade.

➔ **AS YOU HEAD WEST** along the river, you'll quickly reach Queens Bridge; pause to reflect on what was once the Yarra Yarra waterfalls, an important meeting place for both the Woiwurrung (Wurundjeri) and the Boonwurrung Peoples. This natural weir marked an important crossing point and is where the Yarra turned from salt to freshwater – the very reason European settlers decided to put down roots at this exact point. And in case you're wondering what happened to the falls, they were unceremoniously blown up with dynamite in 1883 to prevent flooding.

⊙ **TAKE THE BIKE LANE** and cross Queens Bridge for a quick detour to the plaque commemorating where the *Enterprize* arrived from Tasmania on 30 August 1835 to settle the city of Melbourne, disregarding the First Nations communities already long-established in the area. Raised flags mark the spot, but perhaps a more poignant landmark at **Enterprize Park** is the art installation *Scar – A Stolen Vision*. Created as a collaboration by First Nation artists, it features 30 poles reclaimed from the bridge and transformed into modern-day scarred trees – the visible reminder from removing a tree's bark to make canoes and shields – with the term 'scar' being a double entendre representing the ongoing process of healing wounds upon what was originally a traditional campground before European settlement.

⊙ **CONTINUE ALONG** the north bank of the Yarra to pass Melbourne's popular **SEA LIFE Aquarium** (visitsealife.com/melbourne), perhaps best saved for a rainy day, and **Blue Tongue Bikes** (bluetonguebikes.com.au) (*see* p16) who can help out with anything from repairs, bike rental and tours. Glide past the helipad (where high-rollers are zipped back and forth) to cross back over the river at **South Wharf**. Carefully weave through crowds of strolling families and couples out on date night all under the shadow of controversial Crown Casino; love it or hate it, you'd find it hard to deny that its restaurants are world-class.

⊙ **AHEAD** is the *Polly Woodside* (nationaltrust.org.au/places/polly-woodside) an old-school Melbourne attraction that's not actually from Melbourne but Belfast: a beautifully preserved 19th-century three-masted iron barque that's sat moored here for many a year. Pass by the Melbourne Convention and Exhibition Centre (better known as Jeff's Shed, after the premier who built it) all while resisting – or giving in to, depending on how much of a hunger you've already worked up – temptations of anything from riverside Thai to German beerhalls till you reach **Webb Bridge**. With its snaking design inspired by a traditional First Nations eel trap, it looks more like an art installation than footbridge, and in keeping with its intended analogy it links old with new as you wind over the river to arrive at the Docklands.

⊘ **THIS SIDE OF THE RIVER** brings a whole new perspective as the bike path bisects **Central Pier** river quay (where ferries depart to Geelong and the Bellarine Peninsula), with Bolte Bridge looming on one side and the AFL Docklands Stadium on the other. Among waterfront cafes and shipping container street-art is **Bike Hub** (goodcycles.org.au/docklands) who can help out with niggly repairs, and best of all, they're on call for 'on-trail' assistance if you get a puncture down the track. And how can we leave here without mentioning that cow snagged upside down in a tree? Created by John Kelly, this photogenic sculpture is one of Dockland's best-known landmarks.

⊘ **PUSHING ALONG**, ignore the wrongly directed sign pointing up La Trobe St and keep on along the Esplanade trail that curves around an industrial highway to hell as you're immersed among belching truck fumes. Thank god for the bike path! Here you'll pass by the much-maligned **Melbourne Star Observation Wheel**, which has been constructed, dismantled and reassembled so many times everyone's lost count! That's if it's even there any more ... it went into liquidation in late 2021, so whether new buyers take it over or it's relocated, we'll have to wait and see. Cross at the lights to clear Footscray Rd for another change of scenery as you join the Moonee Ponds Creek Trail.

⊘ **SKIRTING ITS NAMESAKE CREEK** the path takes you down a gritty trail mixing industry, train yards and graffiti-spattered underpasses, all offset by this Yarra tributary, where conservation efforts are slowly attempting to beautify and biodiversify by creating a habitat to bring back native species. Keep on going for another 3.5km till you see Flemington Bridge train station, where you'll need to shift down to first gear and head up the steep path (unsigned – grrr!) and over a bridge passing across the tolled highways to join the relaxed, nature-filled stretch along the Upfield path. Here the trail runs alongside the train tracks as you leave the traffic behind to find

yourself among native grasses and ancient lava flows embedded in sandstone at Royal Park Railway Cutting. Further ahead, take the detour left to **Trin Warren Tam-Boore**, an urban wetlands precinct in the heart of the city with a boardwalk and bird hide overlooking the reed-filled waterhole. It's also the habitat of the rare White's skink, which has chosen (poorly?) a former rubbish tip as its last stronghold in Melbourne. From here you'll hit the green belt of aptly named Parkville, home to the expansive **Royal Park** (where Burke and Wills set off on their ill-fated expedition) and Australia's oldest zoo, **Melbourne Zoo** (`zoo.org.au/melbourne`).

⊜ **GET READY** to be frustrated again by a lack of signage as you reach a fork in the road at Royal Park train station. Cross at the boom gates and keep riding up and around the platform to join the Inner Circle Rail Trail. If you ever wondered why Fitzroy and Carlton don't have a train line, the answer is that they used to till 1948 before the popularity of trams made this line obsolete. But it's the tracks of the defunct railway you're now following as you pass through Princes Park and the only remaining station building of North Carlton, since converted into a Neighbourhood House.

At this point you may notice a distinct shift in demographic as suddenly there's less lycra and more flannel shirts, Nudie jeans and tattoos, all while pushies replace road bikes to signify you've reached Melbourne's cool inner-north suburbs. For a bit of an off-trail detour, you can take a quick left at Lygon St to check out **East Brunswick**'s happening strip of bars, cafes and multicultural restaurants

⊜ **BY THIS STAGE** you'll have worked up a thirst, so it's a perfect time to reach **Park St** (`parkstreetdining.com.au`), a hip little cafe conveniently located on the bike path with top-notch coffee, sandwiches and local beers to enjoy at its outdoor or indoor seating, depending on the weather (and how sweaty you are). Next door is **Velo Cycles** (`velocycles.com.au`) who likewise smartly opened along the Capital Trail to offer bike rental, accessories and repairs. If you're around on Sunday morning, get in touch with `neighbourlyride.com` for social rides leaving from here at 10am.

⊙ **THEN IT'S BACK ON THE BIKE** – no doubt with a sore bum and feeling a bit sluggish post-feed – to continue through the parklands of hipster North Fitzroy, passing the imposing red-brick heritage-listed old electric railway substation. Reaching Rushall station, where again crucial directions go missing, head down the trail underpass to land yourself on **Merri Creek Trail** (p84) for one of the day's highlights with its dense bush-lined creek trail with long breezy downhills.

⊙ **IT SETS THE SCENE** for what's to come as you continue on through to **Yarra Bend Park**, passing community initiatives like Merri Creek labyrinth and historical sites such as the 19th-century Merri Creek Aboriginal School before reaching **Dights Falls**. This is where Merri Creek joins the Yarra, a famous landmark river bend worthy of a stop for a few snaps and to take in the natural landscapes of this beloved confluence. For many thousands of years this has been an important meeting spot for the Wurundjeri People to hunt for local game and fish and gather for corroborees and ceremonies, as well as crossing the river along a basalt rock weir. It's the burial place of Billibellary (uncle to William Barak), a revered Elder and leader of the Wurundjeri-willam clan. But today it's not so much 'falls' as a somewhat underwhelming artificial weir, originally built in 1895 to provide water for the a local flour mill before being replaced in 2012 to boost the native fish population, which may explain the number of anglers out here dropping a line.

⊙ **HERE'S AROUND THE HALFWAY MARK** and it's not a bad place to take a break, with some lovely picnic spots, including Studley Park Boathouse (`studleyparkboathousekew.com.au`): the pick of them all. It's Melbourne's oldest boathouse where you can have your *Wind in the Willows* moment as you go for a leisurely row. But it's probably more a cold drink you're after, in which case head to its elegant Edwardian restaurant looking out over a bushy bend in the river where, just across from here, was the site of Yarra Bend Lunatic Asylum.

⊙ **FROM HERE** you're on the Main Yarra Trail for the remainder of the journey, passing a colourful 90m-long mural painted by street artist Tom Civil in conjunction with the Wurundjeri People featuring motifs from both local natural scenery and First Nations cultures. Your legs will enjoy this scenic downhill stretch of pristine river lined with paperbarks and river red gums that'll have you wondering if you're really still in Melbourne. And even more so as you next come across grazing sheep, goats and dairy cattle – a telltale sign you've arrived at **Collingwood Children's Farm** (farm.org.au). A much-loved inner-city treasure, this is one for kids and adults alike, where it's as much about petting goats as it is all about community, not-for-profit permaculture and organic farming and a cafe (farmcafe.com.au) that's perfect for afternoon tea of scones with jam and cream.

Just up from the farm is another local institution in the **Abbotsford Convent** (abbotsfordconvent.com.au), a former nunnery dating from the 1850s. Today it's a vibrant arts precinct where you can do a self-guided tour of its austere historic architecture all while taking in current-day creative vibes and food stops such as the Convent Bakery (conventbakery.com), which uses wood-fired masonry ovens dating to 1901 to bake rustic and organic artisanal breads to go with a full cafe menu and good coffee.

⊙ **PUSHING ALONG** through the pastoral landscapes, soon you're back again hugging the banks of the Yarra to arrive at a steep set of stairs where you'll need to lug your bike up, take a breather, and then make your way over the Yarra across the narrow Collins Bridge. Stick to the paved trail to ride alongside Yarra Blvd while staying on the shared bike–pedestrian sidewalk for what's a sweaty climb, before rejoining the bush-lined path for a steep downhill and another bridge crossing where you'll meet again with the river like a long-lost friend.

⊙ **KEEP AN EYE OUT** to your right to spot another of Melbourne's idiosyncratic cultural icons: the **Skipping Girl**, a neon rooftop sign for vinegar on which Little Audrey has been skipping since 1936. She's such a well-known part of the city there's even an indie rock band named after her. Beer lovers take note: there are plenty of microbreweries inland from the river: Moon Dog, Mountain Goat, Burnley Brewing, or if you're not into craft, the oldest of them all, CUB (offering brewery tours, too: `carltonbrewhouse.com.au/pages/brewery-tours`), which has been producing Aussie classics – Foster's, VB, Melbourne Bitter, Carlton Draught – since 1907. Don't go crazy; remember to stay under the limit!

➲ **FROM HERE** you'll feel the burn for what's an undeniably beautiful but loooong stretch without any real stops, as you make your way through Richmond and Hawthorn's endless parkland, prestigious schools, rowing clubs and beautiful houses. But if you think the houses here are nice, wait till you see the hilltop mansions along South Yarra's riverfront! These extravagant mansions are juxtaposed with the swampy **Grange Road Wetlands**, which makes for a peaceful little break, with a boardwalk leading among a sanctuary for native birds, reptiles and wildlife, all accompanied by an audio tour that you can tune into from the QR code.

If you've given your bike a thrashing by this stage, you're in luck as nearby there is a public bike pump and repair station, but it's probably you who needs a little maintenance. Fortunately **Kanteen** (`facebook.com/ontheyarra`) is here – the perfect spot to pull in for a break and cuppa overlooking **Herring Island** (`parks.vic.gov.au/places-to-see/parks/herring-island`); a contender for Melbourne's best-kept secret, where on weekends from January to Easter, a punt makes the trip across the river to allow those interested to explore its sculpture park.

⚑ **FROM HERE YOU'LL** continue along a scenic stretch of the Yarra before finishing with a flourish of Melbourne's icons: the Nylex Clock (p116); the Melbourne Cricket Ground (p112); the Tan, the track originally for exercising horses that have long since given way to walkers and runners (former Olympian Craig Mottram still holds the record at 10 minutes and 8 seconds); and Royal Botanical Gardens as you cruise along the grassy banks of the Yarra, where Melburnians gather for barbecues as the city's skyline looms ahead. Passing a succession of heritage-listed boathouses, you'll zip under Princes Bridge to arrive back at Southbank's riverside precinct to complete the ride at your choice of **Ponyfish Island** (`ponyfishisland.com.au`) or **Riverland** (`riverlandbar.com`), a bluestone bar across on the Yarra's bank, before heading up to Federation Square to finish at Flinders Street station.

Local Chit-chat with Daisy Smith

Daisy Smith is the Community Engagement Ranger with Parks Victoria at the Burnley depot. They operate vessels, including the *Pelican*, which remove litter from numerous traps located along the Yarra and Maribyrnong rivers.

What does the Yarra mean to you?

'Birrarung' is the traditional name of the Yarra River; and 'marr' refers to the mist that sometimes settles over the Birrarung, so, loosely, the words are often translated to 'river of mists'. Birrarung is part of the cultural landscape in the traditional Country of the Wurundjeri Woiwurrung People. I acknowledge and respect the Traditional Custodians and their deep and continuing spiritual connection to the land and waters, and their Elders past and present, whose knowledge and wisdom has ensured the continuation of culture and traditional practices and their unique ability and ongoing role in caring for Country. *'Wilip-gin Birrarung murron'* translates as 'keep the Birrarung alive' in Woiwurrung; through partnership with Traditional Custodians and Aboriginal communities I hope to be able to assist in the protection of Country and continuation of their spiritual and cultural practices for all future generations.

Do you have a favourite section of the Yarra?

The waters around Abbotsford when the sun is rising. You could easily believe you're the only human for miles: all you can see is lush vegetation, and *marr* materalising on the water with the echo of beautiful birdsongs ringing around you. The best way to experience the river is by canoe or kayak! The river is teeming with fish, which attract the sporadic seal affectionately named Salvatore. Dolphins have also been sighted in the river!

Tell us a little bit about Herring Island.

Herring Island Environmental Sculpture Park is a small, 3.2-ha artificial island, home to a series of environmental sculptures interwoven into the park's landscape. The island forms an environmental corridor of wildlife and regional vegetation, consisting of native forest and grassland communities and is home to a variety of birds and other animals, including possums, lizards, and snakes.

With a grassy picnic area, which contains free electric barbecues, drinking fountains, picnic shelters and nearby toilet facilities, the island is the perfect location to spend a day out in nature.

CLICK, READ, LISTEN AND WATCH:

- 🌐 emelbourne.net.au
- 📖 Sophie Cunningham, *Melbourne*
- 🎵 Paul Kelly and the Coloured Girls, 'Leaps and Bounds'
  Painters and Dockers, 'Boy Who Lost his Jocks at
      Flinders St Station'
  Underground Lovers, 'Rushall Station'
  Weddings, Parties, Anything, 'Meet under the Clocks'

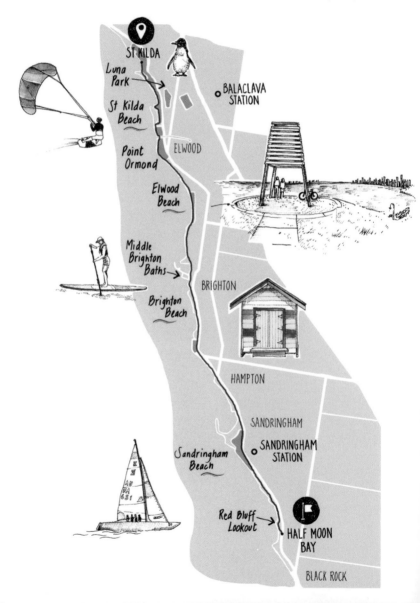

BAY TRAIL: ST KILDA TO HALF MOON BAY

ST KILDA

Luna Park

St Kilda Beach

BALACLAVA STATION

Point Ormond

ELWOOD

Elwood Beach

Middle Brighton Baths

BRIGHTON

Brighton Beach

HAMPTON

SANDRINGHAM

Sandringham Beach

SANDRINGHAM STATION

Red Bluff Lookout

HALF MOON BAY

BLACK ROCK

START
St Kilda

FINISH
Half Moon Bay

DISTANCE
13km one-way

DURATION
2-3 hours return

TRANSPORT
Balaclava is the closest
station. If you're not keen
on the return ride, take
the train from Sandringham
station. You can arrive by
ferry (stkildaferry.com.au)
from Williamstown, but call
ahead to reserve a spot for
your bike. Parking is either
exorbitantly priced or near
impossible to find.

CONNECTING RIDES
Bay Trail extension
to Port Melbourne or
Seaford

Peninsula Link Trail

Elster Creek Trail

A ride through Melbourne's seaside suburbs takes
in Port Phillip Bay/Nerm's local environment,
Yalukit-willam history, 19th-century heritage and
public art, in between plenty of good food and dips
in the bay's string of pretty beaches. In Meyer
Eidelson's *Yalukit Willam: The River People of
Port Phillip*, it is explained that the region
known as Port Phillip Bay is called Nerm, while
the greater Melbourne region is called Naarm.

GROUND ZERO FOR MELBOURNE'S BIKE SCENE, Beach Road has long been known as the place where lycra-clad cyclists come to fly through these bayside suburbs like it's the Tour de Melbourne. And while that's great if you've got all the latest gear and custom-made high-performance bikes, for everyday cyclists like us, the idea of riding among a peloton can seem, quite frankly, a little off-putting. But the good news is that there's a much more leisurely alternative to being caught up in a pack of MAMILs (yes, you know the term: middle-aged man in lycra), and that's where the scenic Bay Trail steps in – a dedicated bike–pedestrian path that runs from Port Melbourne (p118) all the way to Seaford. But the more leisurely St Kilda to Half Moon Bay section is perfect if you don't want to commit to the full 50km.

🚲 **CYCLING WITH KIDS:** Pack your bathers (and maybe a snorkel). For a fun way to kick things off, consider coming via the Williamstown ferry or start at **Luna Park.** Read about First Nations cultures and see artworks, including the Solar System trail. Park the bikes anywhere to feel the sand between your toes, such as at Brighton's **bathing boxes. Half Moon Bay** has a shipwreck and is a wonderful spot for a dip and a snorkel.

📍 **IF THERE'S ANYWHERE** in Melbourne that's more picturesque and festive than **St Kilda Foreshore** on a sunny day, then we'd love to hear about it. Come summer, it's a scene to rival LA's Venice Beach as joggers, walkers, skaters, cyclists and beachgoers descend on the area among revellers and diners here to enjoy the sunshine – all to the balmy backdrop of palm trees and sparkling bay waters where kiteboarders and paddlers are out lapping it up.

➡ **ROLL DOWN** to the grassy St Kilda foreshore passing the 19th-century **Royal Melbourne Yacht Squadron** (rmys.com.au) and the **Captain Cook Memorial**, a statue that was erected back in 1914 and today is semi-regularly targeted by activists calling for a more balanced and reconciliatory retelling of historical events. This is an area where the Yalukit-willam People have resided for tens of thousands of years, and to learn more about this clan of the Boonwurrung People, download the **Indigenous Coastal Trail** (bayside.vic.gov.au/news/indigenous-coastal-trail) for a map detailing interesting stops along the ride.

While the foreshore's most iconic local landmark, **St Kilda Pier** (parks.vic.gov.au/places-to-see/parks/st-kilda-pier-and-breakwater), is more than likely to still be undergoing redevelopment, ordinarily you can pedal out along its walkway that juts 450m out to the bay. Its endpoint rewards with the quaint Edwardian **kiosk** originally dating to 1859, which, after burning down in 2003 in an arson attack, has been faithfully rebuilt. It sits alongside a breakwater that's famous for its **little penguin colony** – come by at dusk later on (around 30 minutes after sunset) where you can usually spot them returning to their burrows. But again, if you do have your heart set on this, to avoid disappointment it's more than likely not to reopen for a few years.

⊜ **BACK ON THE PROMENADE**, stop to admire the pier mosaic by the late **Mirka Mora** (1928–2018), a much-loved artist and local identity whose legacy burns bright with this vibrant ode to St Kilda. And as soon as you hit the beach, you'll pass by **St Kilda Sea Baths** (stkildaseabaths.com.au), a rebuilt version of a historic Spanish Moorish-style building that originally dates to the 1860s and was used to provide single-sex bathing at a time when swimming in the open sea was considered both immoral and dangerous. Today it comprises a much less prudish version, one where (shock, horror!) males and females are allowed in the same indoor heated seawater pool. It's all part of a complex comprising beachfront restaurants and a **kiteboarding school** (kiterepublic.com.au), which offers lessons if you find yourself envious of those radical dudes landing gnarly tricks out on the water.

⊜ **AS YOU CYCLE BY** the grassy foreshore, where the **St Kilda Festival** (stkildafestival.com.au) kicks into action each February, the golden sands of **St Kilda Beach** open up. And while it may not be in the same league as a Bondi or Copacabana, if you ask us, it's pretty glorious all the same. It's a beach that's literally cleaned up its act (with mechanical beach cleaners coming in daily) so the days of fearing to tread on needles here are fortunately in the past. As for whether it's safe to swim here, our advice is to check the Environmental Protection Authority website (epa.vic.gov.au), which offers an accurate and up-to-date advisory on water quality, but the hot tip you'll get from Melburnians is to avoid bay swimming anytime in the 24 to 48 hours after heavy rain.

If you're feeling peckish or thirsty at this point, among the old-school kiosks selling hot chips, ice-cream and cold drinks, you'll find more upmarket options at institutions like **Stokehouse** (stokehouse.com.au/melbourne), rebuilt after also burning down in 2014, and **Donovans** (donovans.com.au) in what was formerly a historic bathing pavilion – both offer beachfront, casual fine dining.

⊜ **PASSING** the St Kilda Life Saving Club (established 1914), don't be alarmed if you hear screaming in the distance; that'll just be the terrified folk riding **Luna Park's** (`lunapark.com.au`) old rickety wooden roller-coaster that dates back to 1912!

🔵 **AS THE BEACH ENDS,** you'll ride around **St Kilda Marina,** which has an octagonal lighthouse for a backdrop. And while we'd love to regale you with tales of all the romance of 19th-century shipwrecks – sorry to break the news but this is not really a lighthouse at all, but rather a fibreglass structure built in the 1960s to look more the part than actually guide in any ships.

🔵 **FROM HERE** the path curves around the marina by the grassy foreshore to reach the suburb of Elwood. Ride over the bridge where **Elwood Canal** (a 1.2-km long waterway constructed in the 19th century upon former swampland) empties into the bay. There's an option for a short off-trail ride along the **Elster** (a German word meaning 'magpie'; hopefully none of which today are in a swooping mood . . .) **Creek Trail** that begins across the road. Along here you can follow scenic inner-city canals that wind by local houses as Melbourne does its best Amsterdam impersonation. Around the corner is **Jerry's Milkbar** (`instagram.com/jerrysmilkbar`), a famed Elwood local cafe, where kids who grew up around here buying $1 bags of mixed lollies are back 30 years later for single-origin coffees and smashed avo.

🔵 **BACK ALONG** the bay the trail passes historical **Point Ormond** – if you thought hotel quarantine was a pain in the arse during Covid, just be thankful you weren't here back in 1840. This here was the site of Victoria's first quarantine station, set up for the arrival of the immigrant ship *Glen Huntly* (which yes, both the road and nearby suburb were named after) that arrived from Scotland carrying passengers sick with typhus. These poor folk weren't fortunate enough to be holed up in comfortable hotel rooms; they spent their first few months in Australia bundled up in cold, wet tents. Today it's marked by a grassy hilltop viewpoint that's the place to come at sunset, and a good spot to reflect on where the Yalukit-willam People would also take up shelter and gather to eat bountiful shellfish feasts.

⊙ **FROM HERE** you'll pass attractive **Elwood Beach** with its century-old **kiosk** (`facebook.com/PointOrmondCafe`), sailing club, surf lifesaving club (the oldest in Victoria, established 1911 before being rebuilt in the '70s) and) and more waterfront dining at **Elwood Bathers** (`elwoodbathers.com`).

⊙ **NEXT** you'll pass a foreshore reserve where you'll get your first look at some prime bayfront real estate as you arrive in la-di-da Brighton, Melbourne's ritziest seaside suburb. There's nowhere better to get a glimpse of how the other half lives than at the 19th-century **Royal Brighton Yacht Club** (`rbyc.org.au`), a club where members look the part with plenty of sweaters over polo shirts and classic cisco shorts to go with boat shoes sans socks (the restaurant, but not the bar, is open to the public). Here's where the Brighton Icebergers meet each morning to set out for their daily swim. They say the water has only three temperatures: 'warm, cold and #@%! freezing', and it's a club that attracts anyone from former premiers to AFL footballers, a group of dedicated swimmers who were the subject of an award-winning short doco *Icebergers* (`icebergersdoco.com`). Alongside the club is **Middle Brighton pier** where you'll cycle out and back again past anglers casting a line as you take in the distant city skyline among pointed masts of moored yachts.

⊜ **ON THE FORESHORE** is the **Middle Brighton Baths**, a beautiful 1936 Art Deco brick building that's divided into a fish-and-chip kiosk and Mod Oz restaurant (middlebrightonbaths.com.au), and the Brighton Baths Health Club (brightonbathshealthclub.com.au): another historic sea bath, this one with outdoor saltwater pool and private beach.

⊜ **HERE** the trail runs by Brighton's Esplanade where grand heritage houses and gaudy McMansions sit side by side on full display. But if you think these are worth a mint, wait until you find what's plonked on the sands of **Brighton Beach** – a very different form of real estate, the Victorian-era **bathing boxes** (brightonbathingbox.org.au), Melbourne icons comprising a row of 82 brightly painted wooden shacks that have sat here for over a century. They are tightly held; it's rare to see one go under the hammer, but when they do, the price is in the vicinity of $350,000, making them Melbourne's most expensive real estate on a per square metre basis – pricey especially given none have electricity or running water. Photographers wanting to get a different shot can head up to Jim Willis Reserve, where you can spot the beach boxes framed by the city skyline. A midden has also been located here where the Yalukit-willam People would cook up their all-you-can-eat shellfish banquets.

And once you've 'done all of Brighton', you'll drift along to under-the-radar Hampton, a laid-back beachside suburb with a long, and often secluded, beach that's popular with kiteboarders. Around here you'll notice local council signs alerting to 'Tree Vandals at Work', which comes with a $20,000 reward – this is a long-fought battle to catch whoever has been poisoning the foreshore vegetation; many suspect it's local residents seeking a better view.

NEXT ALONG is Sandringham, where you'll pass by its footy ground named after the former high-flying Saint, Trevor Barker, and the **Sandringham Croquet Club** – surely it's only a matter of time before hipsters embrace this game to be ironic. The trail skirts by **Sandringham Beach,** a very good choice if you're looking for a dip, before passing the rather grand-looking **Sandringham Band Rotunda** (c. 1926). From here there's a bit of an uphill slog as you ride by Beach Rd, where the lycra brigade fly down at breakneck speed. Pull into the **Red Bluff Lookout** to check out the views and the **Bunjil's Eggs** sculpture, a work by renowned artist Glenn Romanis that comprises six emu eggs representing the six clans of the Boonwurrung People. And along the ride, keep an eye out for the **Bayside Coastal Art Trail** featuring works by prominent Australian Impressionists who have painted these very landscapes you look out to.

NEXT you'll reach the lovely-named **Half Moon Bay,** where you'll dismount to make your way down the steep Cerebus Way passing Black Rock Jetty and its sailing club, before settling in for a well-earned drink at the **Cerberus Beach House** (cerberusbeachhouse.com.au). Here you can choose between the kiosk or licensed restaurant overlooking the wreck of **HMVS *Cerberus*** that was scuttled here in 1926. Built in 1868, though it never saw battle, the *Cerberus* was regarded as one of the world's most innovative and powerful warships of its time and remains the last breastwork monitor class in existence – albeit in a very rusty and broken-up state.

Given you've come all this way it's worth going for a bit of a beach stroll or even a dip in the waters of Half Moon Bay, before it's back on the bike. You have a few options now: you can keep on going all the way to Seaford; take the return ride to St Kilda; or head to Sandringham station where you can jump on a train home. But if you do opt to ride back to St Kilda, the downhill sections make it a bit easier and you'll be treated to wonderful vistas as the city comes into view.

FINISHING BACK in St Kilda, what better place to mark your return than a sunset drink at the **Esplanade Hotel** (`hotelesplanade.com.au`). Hang around for a pub meal, a cocktail in its rather refined upstairs bar (a spare change of clothes may come in handy) or check out who's playing at the Gershwin Room, all while being very pleased to see the Espy – despite the slick makeover – still remains one of St Kilda's very best.

Local Chit-chat with Fam Charko

Fam is an award-winning marine biologist (MSc) with the Port Phillip EcoCentre (`ecocentre.com`) and contributes to research on the health of Melbourne's big rivers and Port Phillip Bay/ Nerm. She is also a scuba instructor and radio host on Radio Marinara – 3RRR (102.7), Sundays 9–10am.

Tell us about Port Phillip EcoCentre and your role there.

We are passionate about supporting people to mitigate and adapt to climate change and to reduce waste and curtail consumption. We do this through citizen science, education, advocacy and developing resilient communities.

My role is that of marine biologist and science communicator. I lead citizen science projects where community members help me collect scientific evidence to use in our advocacy efforts to create positive change for the environment.

How can people get involved?

By becoming part of the EcoCentre family! Become a member (which is free), sign up to volunteer or participate in one of our many community events.

As a scuba diver who's explored many parts of the world, what is unique to Port Phillip Bay/Nerm?

One of the most interesting features is how many species we have in the bay that occur only in the area of Southern

Australia. We have a unique dolphin subspecies here, the Burrunan dolphin, who was only discovered as a genetically different group in 2011. Then there are the weedy seadragons, who float around under piers and jetties, gliding through the water seemingly without effort and drifting on the currents.

But what I really appreciate about the bay is that even though more than 5 million people live right on the banks, we still have all of this richness and beauty right under our noses. We need to keep cherishing and caring for what we still have now, so we don't lose it.

Where would you recommend snorkellers and divers head out in Melbourne's waters?

Just off the big beacon on the hill at Elwood beach, there is a rocky reef that is fun to snorkel in the right conditions. Go there when the tide is half full, and enjoy seeing toadfish, sea stars, sponges, abalone and globefish, as well as a host of colourful algae. It's like a rocky underwater garden. You might get lucky and see the occasional eagle ray and schools of snapper passing through.

Going south just a little bit, you'll find Ricketts Point Marine Sanctuary. It is a haven for marine life, as fishing is prohibited, and one of the best snorkel spots in the bay. You can encounter various species of beautiful stingrays, the small and docile Port Jackson shark, dusky morwong, garfish, flathead and zebra fish. Under the ledges of the rocky reef you can see cold-water sponges and hard corals that come in fluoro green, blue and orange colours.

In Black Rock, spot big-belly seahorses holding onto the rungs of the pier's ladder with their tails.

On the Mornington Peninsula in winter, thousands of giant spider crabs go on the march into the shallows to form large crab mounds before they moult simultaneously and disappear back into the depths again. They were featured in BBC's *Blue Planet II* by Sir David Attenborough and divers from all over the world travel here to witness this amazing natural phenomenon.

Outside the water, what are some of your favourite things to do around Melbourne's bay suburbs?

I love taking friends and overseas visitors to see the colony of little penguins on the St Kilda breakwater. In the summer months, after sunset, you can watch the penguins come in to feed their chicks and socialise with their neighbours. That we can witness something like this so close to the city is something I will never take for granted.

CLICK, READ, LISTEN AND WATCH:

- 🌐 bayside.vic.gov.au/services/trees-parks-and-beaches/ coastal-trails
- 📖 Meyer Eidelson, *Yalukit Willam: The River People of Port Phillip (2014)*
- 🎵 Paul Kelly, 'From St Kilda to Kings Cross'
  Amanda Palmer & The Grand Theft Orchestra, 'From St. Kilda To Fitzroy'
  The Cat Empire, 'The Crowd'
  The Lucksmiths, 'The Sandringham Line'

HOBSONS BAY COASTAL TRAIL

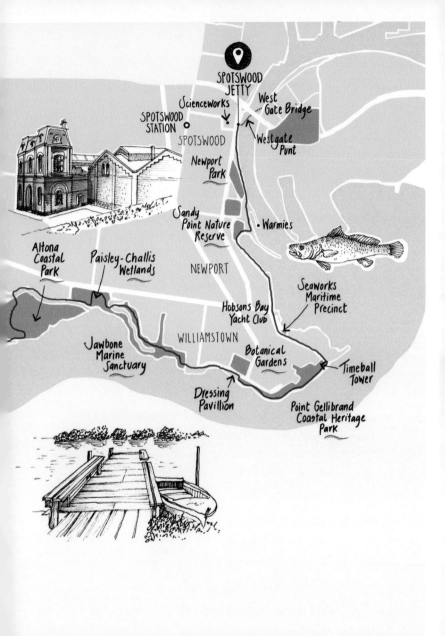

SPOTSWOOD JETTY

Scienceworks

West Gate Bridge

SPOTSWOOD STATION

SPOTSWOOD

Westgate Punt

Newport Park

Warmies

Sandy Point Nature Reserve

NEWPORT

Altona Coastal Park

Paisley-Challis Wetlands

Seaworks Maritime Precinct

Hobsons Bay Yacht Club

WILLIAMSTOWN

Jawbone Marine Sanctuary

Botanical Gardens

Timeball Tower

Dressing Pavillion

Point Gellibrand Coastal Heritage Park

START
Spotswood Jetty

FINISH
Skeleton Creek,
Altona Meadows

DISTANCE
23km one-way

DURATION
4 hours return

TRANSPORT
From Spotswood station it's a short ride to the trail; otherwise take the Westgate Punt from Fishermans Bend. To return, you can take the train from Altona station. On weekends, ferries run from Williamstown to St Kilda via Port Melbourne.

CONNECTING RIDES
Bay Trail

Federation Trail

Maribyrnong River Trail (p74)

Skeleton Creek Trail

Though just a short jaunt across from Melbourne's CBD, a trip out to Hobsons Bay feels like an old-fashioned seaside holiday, with fish and chips by the beach and strolls along the jetty with ice-cream in hand. This family-friendly trail is the perfect way to spend a Sunday as you soak up ye olde maritime atmosphere. And this being where the Yarra River meets the ocean, you'll pass coastal reserves and pristine wetlands, making this a wonderful ride for nature lovers, too.

THERE ARE TWO WAYS OF GETTING HERE: the boring way or the fun way, so no prizes in guessing which choice we prefer. And though driving or taking the train to Spotswood is by far the easiest, our advice is to take a punt – both literally and figuratively – and hop aboard the Westgate Punt (westgatepunt.com). This one-off boat ride will give you a very different perspective as you and your bike are ferried across this industrial bend of the Yarra to pass directly beneath the hulking **West Gate Bridge.** Setting out from Lorimer St 'Beach' in Port Melbourne, the punt departs every 30 minutes to deliver you to Spotswood Jetty, the official start of the Hobsons Bay Coastal Trail. To get there, you can ride via the Lorimer bike path that connects it to the city.

🚲 **CYCLING WITH KIDS:** Start with a mini adventure as you take the punt and arrive at **Scienceworks.** Explore the maritime museum and pirate-themed tavern in **Williamstown's Seaworks** Maritime Precinct. At **Altona Beach** stroll out along the pier with an ice-cream, and maybe take the train back to Spotswood. If you continue, the **Cheetham Wetlands** have birdlife galore.

⬤ **JUST BEFORE** you pedal off, take note of that historical red-brick French Renaissance-style building that sits across the road. This here is the old **Spotswood Pumping Station** (c. 1890) where Melbourne's (or 'Smellbourne's' as it was known back in the day) sewage passed through en route to the Werribee treatment works (aka the Werribee poo farm) right up until 1965. And though you won't find any garish yellow Interceptors parked out front, fans of the original *Mad Max* (1979) film will also recognise it as the site of the headquarters of the Main Force Patrol. It makes up part of the **Scienceworks Museum** (museumsvictoria.com.au/scienceworks) complex, a hands-on interactive science museum that's well worth a look if you have little ones in tow. And if you're feeling peckish, drop by **Grazeland** (grazeland. melbourne), a 'playground for foodies' that comes alive on weekends with food trucks, bars and live music – but that's one best left till to the end.

⬤ **ONCE YOU'RE DONE** looking around, the trail kicks off along the waterfront to pass **Riverside Park** where you'll learn about the area's historic timber wharves and docks, before arriving at **Newport Park** – home to what in 1950s was the largest power station in the southern hemisphere. And as bleak and Cold War-era as that all sounds, remarkably it's still operational today (run by EnergyAustralia) but rather than coal these days it's all gas-powered. Check out that heritage-listed Edwardian-era gatehouse before moving along to the **HMAS *Yarra* Memorial** to pay respects to the 138 men who lost their lives in World War II at the hands of Japanese warships. Remarkably 13 crew members did survive; they floated out at sea for five days before being rescued by a Dutch submarine south of Java, Indonesia.

⬤ **A BIT FURTHER AHEAD** is where the Yarra River's long, winding journey comes to an end as it feeds into the open waters of Port Phillip Bay/Nerm. This is a fishing hotspot known as the **Warmies**, where the local saying goes 'If the stack's blowing, I know where I'm going' – a reference to the heated waters discharged from Newport Power Station that attract mulloway, tailor and salmon among other species (but hopefully none of the three-eyed variety with the questionable water quality).

Sandy Point Nature Reserve is also here, a gated nature trail where you can cycle out among protected saltmarsh mudflats and woodlands overlooking Greenwich Bay, home to many waterbirds for twitchers to tick off their lists.

⊙ **AND THEN** it's on to Williamstown, one of Victoria's first European settlements. Named William's Town in honour of King William IV, it makes a grand first impression as you pedal down the Strand's ritzy waterfront esplanade to see how the other half lives. It's home to some of Melbourne's prime real estate: a mix of elegant Victorian-era heritage and contemporary architecture, a contrast that confounds as much as it dazzles. But long before the rich people moved in, this foreshore was all she-oak scrub, which led the Yalukit-willam People – who have resided in Melbourne's bay area for millennia – to name it Koort-boork-boork, which translates as 'clump of she-oaks'.

⊙ **CONTINUE ALONG** the foreshore reserve to Williamstown Sailing Club where you can tinker away at any niggling last-minute adjustments at the public bike repair station with pump and tools. Look out for the plaque dedicated to the one million Irish people who died during the Great Famine from 1845 to 1852 and the dispossessed survivors who sailed here to Hobsons Bay to start a new life. Further along is another waterfront park where you'll see several mounted 19th-century cannons placed here to repel a possible Russian attack, and a reminder that the Victoria Navy based here in Williamstown was, in fact, Australia's first.

⊙ **NEXT ALONG** is the Art Deco **Hobsons Bay Yacht Club** (est. 1888) that sits at the roundabout leading into Williamstown's main drag for local amenities, pubs and cafes. Continue along the bay trail to pass heritage-listed boatbuilders, including the fifth-generation **Blunt Boats** (bluntboats.com.au) who have been at it here since the 1850s; you're welcome to pop by to say g'day and see what they're building.

You're now at Williamstown's waterfront dining precinct with all manner of restaurants, cafes and bars along a monumental goldrush-era streetscape that looks straight out of a movie set.

⊙ **THE TRAIL PASSES BY** the expansive Commonwealth Reserve where you'll find the super helpful **Hobsons Bay Visitor Information Centre** (hobsonsbay.vic.gov.au/visit/home) from where you'll make a detour to **Gem Pier** for sparkling views of yacht-filled marinas and the city's cosmopolitan skyline across the bay. On weekends you can take the Coastal Flyer (stkildaferry.com.au) across the bay to St Kilda via Port Melbourne, but call ahead if you're travelling by bike. **HMAS Castlemaine** (hmascastlemaine.org.au) is also docked here. Like many historical warships, it was built right here in Williamstown. On weekends you can clamber aboard the World War II corvette to explore this vessel that was attacked by Japanese bombers in Darwin in 1942.

For a more current-day battle being waged, stop by **Sea Shepherd Australia** (seashepherd.org.au) to get a rundown on their 40-year eco-campaign at their headquarters located on Ann St Pier. This all makes up part of the fascinating **Seaworks Martime Precinct** (seaworks.com.au) that includes the Maritime Museum, which tells the area's seafaring history, an arr-matey pirate-themed tavern and the sobering bluestone Williamstown Morgue where the deceased were hung from the rafters to avoid being eaten by rats!

⊙ **FROM HERE** the trail winds around the bend to deliver a different change of scenery as you arrive at **Point Gellibrand Coastal Heritage Park**. The ocean opens up before you as you take the salty windswept path lined with information boards detailing Point Gellibrand's rich heritage. Here it reads: 'You are now standing at the most important site in the history of Victoria', which, while it is true in the context of this being Victoria's first permanent non-First Nations settlement, it's important to note that the Yalukit-willam People had gathered here for many thousands of years prior to John Batman's arrival in 1835. Point Gellibrand's most iconic landmark is here, the bluestone **Timeball Tower**. And what's a timeball tower I hear you ask? Very good question!

It's an archaic maritime navigational system that allowed ships in the harbour to set their chronometers in accordance to position of the copper ball that was dropped daily from the tower's mast at 1pm on the dot. This one was originally built as a lighthouse in 1849 (making it one of Victoria's oldest) before it became a timeball tower from 1861 to 1926 – and today it remains one of the few operational timeball towers (as a historical demonstration, that is) found in the world; an event you can still witness at 1pm each day.

And while today Hobsons Bay is all about luxury yachts out on the water, things here weren't always so rosy. Spare a thought for those poor souls shackled aboard Melbourne's notorious 19th-century prison hulks, a series of floating gaols with a horrific reputation that sat anchored 100m offshore at Point Gellibrand. The only remnant today is an anchor from one of the hulks located at the Timeball Tower.

⊙ **CONTINUING ALONG** you'll pass the historic remains of 19th-century Fort Gellibrand locked behind a fence, before passing one of Melbourne's most scenic footy grounds with its ocean backdrop and where Williamstown Seagulls have played VFA (now the VFL) games since the 1860s. You'll then pass the **Williamstown Botanical Gardens** – one of Victoria's oldest – which you can enter through ornate front gates on Giffard St. Otherwise continue along the trail and admire the truly superb heritage-listed houses along this side of the esplanade.

⊙ **JUST WHEN YOU THINK YOU'RE DONE** with Williamstown, its glorious beach appears, with its enticing soft sand that makes it a contender as one of Melbourne's best. And what better Aussie tradition is there than fish and chips by the beach? Take your choice between the Rotunda or the Kiosk by d'Asporto (facebook.com/thekioskdasporto) as you shoo off scavenging seagulls trying to pinch your chips. For something more upmarket, Sebastians (sebastianbeachgrill.com) is set inside the heritage-listed **Williamstown Dressing Pavilion**, a beautiful European Modernist–style building dating to the 1930s.

⊖ **FROM HERE** the trail moves along to the more rural landscape of **Jawbone Marine Sanctuary** (jawbone.org.au), a 30-ha reserve with over 2km of protected coastal area comprising sub-tidal basalt reefs, mangroves and mudflats. Its scenic estuarine wetlands (a former rifle range, in case you're wondering) provide a habitat for varied birdlife, with some 160 species recorded both here and further along at **Paisley–Challis Wetlands.** Passing around Maddox Rd, the trail runs by the heritage-listed **Kororoit Creek Fishing Village**, a ramshackle, and kinda creepy, collection of old fishing shacks and boat sheds dating from the 1920s.

⊖ **AT THIS POINT** you'll leave Williamstown to arrive at the vast **Altona Coastal Park.** Today it serves as important conservation area protecting native habitat and waterbirds, but back in the day it was used as the Cut-Paw-Paw Sanatorium, an infectious disease hospital built in the 1880s to quarantine outbreaks of anything from smallpox to the bubonic plague. Remember when a pandemic was an olden-day thing? This is also the site of the former Williamstown racecourse, where Phar Lap won the Underwood Stakes in 1931. And speaking of Australian racing champions, a bit further ahead is the turn off to **Cherry Lake** (a 1.5km detour along the bike path) where in the 1950s, there was a motor-racing track where F1 world champion Jack Brabham set the lap record in his Cooper T23 Bristol in 1954. Instead of race cars, today it's all pelicans, swans and windsurfers among those picnicking by its picturesque shore. But unless you have energy to burn, it's not an essential stop, so feel free to continue on through the **P.A. Burns Reserve** conservation area where dogs run amok on its popular off-leash beach.

⊖ **ZIPPING BY** Altona Yacht Club and Seaholme Jetty, next up you'll find yourself cruising along Altona's scenic esplanade lined with heritage-listed Norfolk Island pines. With its wide swathe of golden sand, **Altona's main beach** is a ripper and its landmark historical 1887 pier is the perfect stop to enjoy an ice-cream. It's a popular kiteboarding spot too, so if the winds are blowing you'll see many kitesurfers out carving it up. Great for the kitesurfers, not so great for cyclists battling a headwind with burning thighs! In summer you can also rent a SUP (stand-up paddleboard) (sunseekersmelbourne.com.au) or sign up for a snorkelling tour (snorkeldivemelbourne.com.au) but that's probably all best left for another day ...

⊘ **AS YOU RIDE ALONG,** the beach gives way to parkland and more wetlands, an area that once was an explosives storage site from 1901 to 1962. Crossing over Laverton Creek bridge, the trail leads through woodland where you can keep an eye out for both the critically endangered swift parrot and the Altona skipper butterfly, which is endemic to this immediate area. Next you'll arrive at **Truganina Park** with more wetlands and its '100 Steps to Federation' walk that leads up to views out over both the You Yangs to the south-west and where the *Time Beacon* sculpture sits representing the past, future and present. But given how far you've come, if 100 steps seem too much for your legs to take, you're forgiven if you just want to keep cycling. Ahead await open grasslands where, remarkably, Australia's first-ever passenger flight took place, back in February 1911 in a Bristol biplane. And by 'passenger' we should clarify it was more a quick fly-around with the pilot and his mate!

⊘ **AND JUST WHEN** fatigue starts to kick in, you'll reach the end of the trail marked by the very Aussie outback-named **Skeleton Creek**, which runs from the far outer western suburb of Tarneit to empty out into Port Phillip Bay/Nerm. Though you're probably 'wetlanded out' by this point, the Ramsar Unesco-listed **Cheetham Wetlands** here are the best of the lot. And if you cycle a little further up to the bridge you can take in its serene natural landscapes, home to many migratory bird species – including the red-necked stint, which despite its diminutive size (small as a sparrow) is an absolute behemoth in the air, embarking on a yearly 26,000km epic voyage from Altona to Siberia and back, passing over Japan, China and Mongolia en route. So stop complaining about your sore bum and achey legs.

⚑ **AND THAT BRINGS TO AN END** what's an eventful, nature-filled, history-packed ride. It's a little intimidating to see just how distant Melbourne's skyline appears from the finishing point, but rest assured: if the return ride's too far to contemplate, you can finish up at Altona station (7km), where regular trains will zip you back to Spotswood.

Local Chit-chat with Max Bohac

Max Bohac is employed at Sea Shepherd Australia's Southern Operation Base in Williamstown.

How long have you been involved with Sea Shepherd?

I have been involved with Sea Shepherd for seven years – two years as a crew member on the ship and five years as an employed member of Sea Shepherd Australia. My role started as office admin and has recently become merchandise coordinator – looking after our merch and merchandise partnerships.

What kinds of campaigns have you been involved in?

I was part of the last Antarctic campaign – Operation Nemesis – where we set out to find and stop the whaling fleet in the Southern Ocean. I also crewed on the Jeedara campaign to stop oil drilling in the Great Australian Bight, and Operation Reef Defence, which took the ship up to the Adani coalmine in Queensland, stopping at strategic points to reach out to communities about this issue and the issue of our reefs dying.

What's there for visitors to see and do when stopping by Sea Shepherd's location there in Williamstown?

Our head office is located in Williamstown at Ann Street. You can always pop into our shop to say hi, buy some merch and have a chat about our frontline ocean-conservation campaigns.

How can visitors get involved in supporting or volunteering at Sea Shepherd?

Anyone wanting to get involved can always become a regular donor to help fund our campaigns, or attend our beach clean-ups – these are always open to the public – or sign up to onshore volunteer with the local chapter.

What are some of your favourite ways to spend your time around Williamstown and the Hobsons Bay area?

I just started snorkelling, so that's been great fun. I probably won't be doing much of that during winter though!

CLICK, READ, LISTEN AND WATCH:

- Hobsons Bay Visitor Information Centre (hobsonsbay.vic.gov.au/visit/Home)
- David Hance, *Sea Shepherd: 40 Years*
- The Orbweavers, 'Spotswood'
- *Mad Max* (1979, directed by George Miller)
  Spotswood (1991, directed by Mark Joffe)

FAIRFIELD TO HEIDE

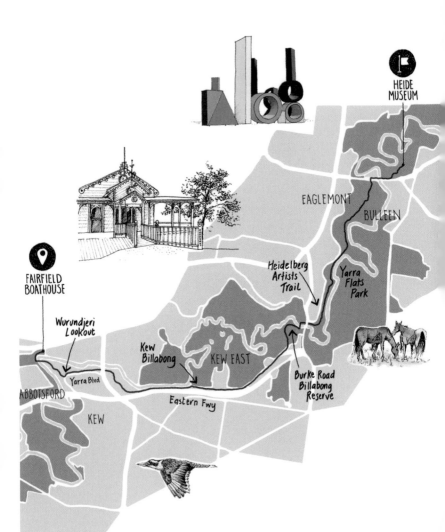

HEIDE MUSEUM

EAGLEMONT

BULLEEN

FAIRFIELD BOATHOUSE

Heidelberg Artists Trail

Yarra Flats Park

Wurundjeri Lookout

Kew Billabong

KEW EAST

Yarra Blvd

Burke Road Billabong Reserve

ABBOTSFORD

Eastern Fwy

KEW

START
Fairfield Boathouse

FINISH
Heide Museum of Modern Art, Bulleen

DISTANCE
10km one-way

DURATION
2–4 hours return

TRANSPORT
Dennis station along the Hurstbridge Line is a 1.5km ride to the trailhead at Fairfield Park. If driving, there's plenty of parking in the vicinity.

CONNECTING RIDES
Main Yarra Trail
Darebin Creek Trail
Koonung Creek Trail
Diamond Creek Trail
Mullum Mullum Creek Trail

This art-themed ride passes through Melbourne's inner-city green belt beside billabongs and river red gums before leading through pastoral landscapes painted by 19th-century Heidelberg School artists. Its endpoint is one of Melbourne's most-loved galleries, the Heide Museum of Modern Art.

LIKE A PICTURE POSTCARD depicting a genteel age of Victoria-era rowboats, ducks and Devonshire tea, the quaint **Fairfield Boathouse** (`fairfieldboathouse.com`) makes for a jolly good start to a bicycle ride. And though these days there's no trace of lacy bonnets, stripy blazers, parasols and boater hats (though don't discount a comeback by Gen Z's fashionistas), all else remains intact along this picturesque river bend with its ornate 110-year-old pavilion and terraced lawns. As tempting as it is to linger, you're here to ride not row a boat, so grab a coffee and get on your bike; those scones will have to wait as your return reward.

🚲 **CYCLING WITH KIDS:** At the **Fairfield Boathouse,** you can hire a rowboat or enjoy scones and cream before setting off. Pack some pencils and a sketchpad; you can seek out a great spot to create your own Impressionist masterpiece. The sculpture garden at **Heide Museum of Modern Art** is perfect for laying out a picnic blanket to enjoy some lunch. Heide offers activities for kids, so check its website to see what's on.

ROLLING DOWN the steep embankment, disembark at the 19th-century **Fairfield Pipe Bridge** (built to bring in water from Yan Yean Reservoir) where you'll wheel your bike across the Yarra and its idyllic outlooks over the boathouse. It's then straight into low gear for what's a short butt-burning climb that rewards with dramatic views from **Wurundjeri Lookout**. This is where Melbourne's skyline meets the bush and it's a pleasant spot to pay your respect to the Wurundjeri People, the Traditional Owners of these beautiful landscapes from where they've fished, camped and held large meetings for at least 30,000 years.

NEXT UP, coast down the shared bike–pedestrian footpath alongside Yarra Blvd to join the **Main Yarra Trail** beneath the heritage-listed lattice truss bridge. And though you're beside the busy Eastern Fwy, any traffic noise is offset by the beauty of the tree-fringed river and one of Melbourne's few surviving billabongs as the sound of kookaburras and rainbow lorikeets echoes about. Wilsmere Park is just ahead if you need a bike repair station with a pump, along with a drinking fountain.

YOU WERE PROMISED a relaxing nature-based ride, but, sorry, the next leg is anything but that. Instead you'll find yourself directly beside the freeway, separated only by a caged barrier as cars scream by at 100km/h. If that's frazzled your nerves, **Burke Road Billabong Reserve** (brbreserve.org) awaits to soothe your soul as you're immersed among its 10-ha pocket of natural bushland, where green thumbs can help dedicated volunteers planting natives.

FROM HERE the path turns to gravel as the scenery becomes distinctly pastoral and, despite being a mere 10km from the city, you'll feel like you're on a country ride as you pinch yourself that somehow you're now riding past horse paddocks and hay bales. This is the beginning of the **Heidelberg Artists Trail**, a bucolic 40km journey through the landscapes that inspired some of Australia's most famous painters: Arthur Streeton, Frederick McCubbin, Tom Roberts, Jane Sutherland and Charles Conder, among prominent Australian Impressionists who made up part of the 19th-century Heidelberg

School. The backstreets just up from here are named Streeton Cres, McCubbin St and the Conder, and at this point along the trail you'll encounter signboards depicting works by these Australian landscape painters from where they set their easels to work.

First up is *Moonrise* by Emanuel Phillips Fox (1865 –1915), a twilight bushscape painted 100m downstream. And after Walter Withers's (1854–1883) lovely *Charterisville Estate* you'll be treated to a hat-trick of Arthur Streeton canvases, most famously, his poetically named *Still Glides the Stream and Shall Forever Glide*: an Impressionist work of the Yarra winding through the countryside with cattle drinking from its banks. Painted in 1890, it's a scene remarkably not too different today. In the background you'll see the Bolin-Bolin Billabong, a wetlands sacred to the Wurundjeri People, and just over the river from here is an area that for many thousands of years was used as a corroboree site and was a rich hunting ground for duck and eel.

There's one remaining painting by Louis Buvelot, considered the father of the Heidelberg School, before these agricultural landscapes come to an end as you loop up a steep path to reach the busy State Route 40. Do a U-turn to leave the Main Yarra Trail (which continues on to Mullum Mullum Creek) to ride along the footpath beside the main road to cross the bridge over the Yarra from where the **Heide Museum of Modern Art** (heide.com.au) – your halfway mark – lies 500m ahead.

⊜ **HERE YOU'LL LEAVE BEHIND** one art movement and move on to the next as you arrive at this arts collective famous for producing Australia's finest 20th-century Modernist and Surrealist painters: Sidney Nolan, Albert Tucker, Arthur Boyd, Charles Blackman, Joy Hester and John Perceval, to name just a few. Set up by art benefactors John and Sunday Reed, who bought a farm here in 1934 to create a hangout for artists, they named it in honour of the Heidelberg School painters who inspired this later crop of artists known as the Heide Circle.

Today, exhibitions display rotating pieces from its permanent collection as well as themed shows relating to both the Heide painters and similar artists. But at this point you're also probably thinking about food, so unless you've packed a picnic, head to the cafe to dine in or, better yet, get takeaway. Make your way down to the beautifully curated grounds – home to wonderful sculpture gardens – and unwind among art-filled surrounds. To uncover added layers of the fascinating history, aim to get here by 11am on Sunday for a tour of the property.

Also take time to visit the beautiful red gum **scarred tree** that's estimated to be 700 years old. Known as Yingabeal (translating in the Woiwurrung language as 'song tree') this is a sacred site to the Wurundjeri People, who used it both to carve out a dugout canoe as well a marker tree, an ancient road sign indicating a travel route. Such routes (known as songlines) involved a fascinating navigational system driven by song used to direct tribes anywhere from hundreds to thousands of kilometres ahead. Yingabeal is believed to be particularly significant in that it guides songlines in five different directions. And just outside Heide you'll find another beautiful marker tree on the corner of Bridge St and Mannigham Rd, albeit at the unenviable location of a petrol station.

⚑ **ONCE YOU'RE DONE HERE**, it's back on the saddle to retrace your tyre tracks to the boathouse. Unless, that is, you're not quite ready to go back yet . . . in which case, if you're fit and raring to go, you can push on to complete the Main Yarra Trail, a route that adds on a further 12km (so basically the same distance you've already come) to bring you to the confluence of the Yarra and Mullum Mullum Creek. It's a ride that passes Lower Plenty over the Ruffey Trail Suspension Bridge where, if you're very lucky, you may spot a platypus. But if all that lazing about in Heide's gardens has you a little sleepy and you're not wild about doing the return leg, a bit further along you can veer off along the Diamond Creek Trail that leads 4km north to Eltham train station.

But otherwise it's another 2.5km ahead to complete the Main Yarra Trail for a truly superb endpoint. As for what happens to the Yarra from here? The scenic journey to its source continues through Warrandyte and the Yarra Valley (Yering, Coldstream, Healesville, Warburton, Reefton and so on) to arrive at the Upper Yarra Reservoir from where the river winding its noble, ancient way through the Yarra Ranges National Park to its headwaters in the foothills of Mt Baw Baw. And for you? Hopefully your art-filled journey has been not only scenic but also inspiring – perhaps enough so to create a masterpiece of the ride? Or at the very least to flop on the couch and post a pic on Insta.

Local Chit-chat with Kendrah Morgan

Kendrah Morgan is head curator at Heide Museum of Modern Art and co-author with Lesley Harding of four books on the history of the museum and artists associated with it: *Sunday's Kitchen: Food and Living at Heide* (2010), *Sunday's Garden: Growing Heide* (2012), *Modern Love: The Lives of John and Sunday Reed* (2015, shortlisted for the Victorian Premier's Literary Award for non-fiction); and *Mirka and Georges: A Culinary Affair* (2018).

Attracting many of Australia's most famous painters (first the Heidelberg School and then the Heide School), what exactly is it about the area that's made it so popular with artists?

This stretch of the Yarra River–Birrarung is very picturesque and in the 1880s and 1890s several Australian Impressionist painters set up artists' camps in the area and produced some of their best-known plein air landscape paintings. Heide founders John and Sunday Reed were well aware of this history when they purchased the Heide property in 1934, and it was no doubt part of its appeal for them. The progressive artists that the Reeds supported and invited to their home also found the local environment beautiful but were of a new generation and drew their inspiration from the European avant-garde movements such as Surrealism and Cubism rather than the landscape.

And as a gallery, what makes Heide so special?

Heide is a living museum with a fascinating history and culturally significant location that makes it unique. As the former home of art patrons John and Sunday Reed, it was witness to a bohemian era involving some of Australian most famous 20th-century artists. Sidney Nolan, for example, who was also Sunday's lover, lived with the Reeds in the early 1940s and painted his iconic Ned Kelly series in the Heide Cottage, where today visitors can soak up the atmosphere and view some of the Reeds' personal art collection. Heide Modern, their award-winning second residence on the property, is equally special, and a space where we honour John and Sunday's legacy with exhibitions by innovative contemporary artists. There are also the larger purpose-built exhibition galleries to enjoy, as well as Heide's beautiful sculpture park and productive gardens, which the Reeds created themselves. Heide is also unique because of its rich First Nations history. A 450-year-old scarred river red gum is said to mark the intersection of five songlines; with our Traditional Owners, we are developing an experiential garden on the river named Yaluk Langa, to tell First Nations stories of the site and local area.

How would you recommend visitors get the most out of a day out to Heide?

There's plenty to do at Heide so ideally allow a few hours for your visit. For first-time visitors I would recommend a Heide History tour by one of our experienced volunteer guides, to learn the backstory to the museum and about the lives of John and Sunday Reed and the artists they championed. See highlights from the museum's collection in Heide Cottage, experience iconic architecture and great art in Heide Modern, and see our headline and subsidiary exhibitions in the main galleries. Stop for coffee breaks or lunch at the Heide Cafe and pick up a reminder of your visit in our fabulous retail store. And save time for a relaxing wander through the sculpture park and down to Yaluk Langa, our First Nations garden in progress by the river.

What else do you recommend people do in the area?

You can cycle from Heide to Bolin Bolin, one of the few remaining billabongs in Melbourne, or visit Banksia and Wombat Bend parks along the river, which have playgrounds and barbecue areas. To explore the history of Australian Impressionist painters in the area follow the Heidelberg Artists Trail, which begins not far from Heide and goes all the way to the Yarra Valley. The miniature railway at nearby Eltham is another local attraction. If you are visiting in the summer you can cool off during your ride at one of the swimming spots along the Birrarung not far from Heide such as Laughing Waters at Eltham or Pound Bend in Warrandyte.

CLICK, READ, LISTEN AND WATCH:

Michael Heyward, *The Ern Malley Affair*
Lesley Harding and Kendrah Morgan, *Modern Love: The Lives of John and Sunday Reed*
Janine Burke, *The Heart Garden: Sunday Reed and Heide*
Angela Hesson and Anne Gray, *She-Oak and Sunlight: Australian Impressionism*

MARIBYRNONG RIVER TRAIL

BRIMBANK PARK

Brimbank Park

EJ Whitten Bridge

Viaduct

Thompson Street Reserve

AVONDALE HEIGHTS

Quang Minh Buddhist Temple

Afton St Conservation Reserve

Maribyrnong Defence Site

Pipemakers Park

MARIBYRNONG

Jack's Magazine

Footscray Park

Flemington Racecourse

FOOTSCRAY

FOOTSCRAY STATION

Heavenly Queen Temple

Footscray Community Arts Centre

MARIBYRNONG ST

START
Maribyrnong St, Footscray

FINISH
Brimbank Park, Keilor East

DISTANCE
23km one-way

DURATION
4–6 hours return

TRANSPORT
From Footscray station it's a short ride to the riverfront trail. From Brimbank Park there's no public transport, so you'll need to commit to the return ride or arrange a pick-up.

CONNECTING RIDES
Capital City Trail (via Dynon Rd) (p28)

Hobsons Bay Coastal Trail (p52)

Steele Creek Trail

Western Ring Road Trail

A 'tale of two rides', this is one of Melbourne's most relaxed bike rides as it follows the meandering Maribyrnong River through the inner-west suburbs before embarking on its middle reaches through natural bushland.

IF THERE'S ONE place people most associate with the western suburbs, it's Footscray, a town with a proud blue-collar heritage, multicultural make-up and no-fuss attitude. From cannoli and bahn mi to injera and samosa, here you'll find all flavours that reflect Footscray's vibrant community. The most recent arrivals have moved across from over the bridge: the young, professional, middle-class. So as you pull into Footscray's newfangled train station to join the start of the trail, it may surprise you to find all these shiny high-rise residential towers in addition to the microbreweries, hipster cafes, bike shops and bars. Keep in mind that before anyone else moved in (including the craft beer-loving hipsters), here along the length of the trail's riverbanks is where the Yalukit-willam and Wurundjeri-willam Peoples have resided for around 30,000.

Footscray was also the home of activist and Yorta Yorta man William Cooper. His house at 73 Southampton Street, Footscray was an early headquarters of the Australian Aborigines' League. It is perhaps most famous as the place from which Cooper walked in protest against Kristallnacht.

🚲 **CYCLING WITH KIDS:** This fairly long ride may be best divided into two. Starting by treating yourself to a cannoli at **T Cavallaro & Sons** and a look around **Footscray Market**. There are plenty of parks and playgrounds along the way; the **Anglers Tavern** has a kids' menu of pizza and nuggets. At the Afton St bridge, assess whether to keep going or save the bushland scenery of the remainder for another day. **Brimbank Park** has plenty of activities, local wildlife and a cafe.

STARTING FROM Maribyrnong St, the trail sets off along disused rail sidings from the historic Footscray wharves; to your left, parkland leads up to the heritage bluestone **Footscray Community Arts Centre** (footscrayarts.com); check out its website for current exhibitions. Just up from here is Hopkins Bridge, where not long ago you'd likely find anti-social activity; today it's all taut-bodied rock climbers showing off their skills on the bouldering wall. Welcome to the new Footscray!

Out of all of Footscray's nicknames, including Foot-scary and Foots-crazy, it's Franco Cozzo's 'Foot-a-scray' that's the most loved and familiar – and fitting given it's an area celebrated for its multiculturalism. It was originally named Mirring-gnai-birr-nong, meaning 'I can hear a ringtail possum', indicative of its abundant wildlife, and a long way from its 19th-century moniker 'Stinkoplis' after the river was duly transformed into a polluted slum of belching factories, wharves and abattoirs refineries – a lot of polluting industries still remain today.

CURVING ROUND the bend, the trail opens to beautifully framed views of the city before the **Heavenly Queen Temple** (heavenlyqueentemple.com.au) appears to your left. This is Australia's largest Taoist Temple, a complex built entirely from donations, and it comprises ornate halls and a 15m-tall statue of the Chinese sea goddess, Mazu, who stands as a picture of serenity, in direct contrast to the whirr of industry across the river.

⊖ **PEDALLING ON**, you'll pass conservation reserves and wetlands, where a lot of hard work has gone into revitalising the local habitat to lure back native aquatic life, waterbirds and reptiles. Across the river **Flemington Racecourse** (`vrc.com.au`) soon comes into view, its track and grandstand an impressive sight; and, of course, it's home to the Melbourne Cup, the race that has been stopping the nation since 1861. To your left are the heritage-listed Edwardian gardens of **Footscray Park**, where punters have gathered at picnics to watch the Cup (or, at least, the bit of the track you can see) for over 100 years.

⊖ **FROM HERE** the trail follows a narrow isthmus that'll have you briefly flanked either side by water and prime riverfront properties where, rather than cars parked out front of the house, they have their boats moored. Returning to the river's west bank, you'll see the compound walls of **Jack's Magazine** (`workingheritage.com.au/places/jack-s-magazine`), Victoria's largest explosive storage facility, built in 1878. There are two vaulted bluestone storage buildings concealed within a grassy blast mound wall designed to withstand any damage if it ever went *KABOOM!* Check the website for when it's open for guided tours. Who's Jack, you ask? Wally Jack, of course: the site keeper whose fiery reputation left all with no uncertain terms as to whose magazine this was!

⊖ **RIDE BY** the Frogs Hollow Wetlands to reach **Pipemakers Park**, an expansive reserve that today is hard to believe was once the area's main industrial hub: first a boiling-down works, then Australia's oldest meat cannery before it became a pipe factory among other things over its 140 years. Here also is the **Living Museum of the West** (`livingmuseum.org.au`) that celebrates the culture and heritage of people from the western suburbs and Maribyrnong River.

There's a bike repair station if you need a tune up before continuing along this ultra-relaxed river trail lined with palm trees that leads to the riverfront **Anglers Tavern** (`anglers-tavern.com.au`), a historic pub dating to the 1860s that's a perfect place to stop for a view and a cold drink.

From here you'll cruise along the waterfront boulevard of Chifley Drive – bonus points to whoever first spots the life-sized giraffe grazing in someone's yard – looking out to Maribyrnong's rowing clubs and parkland before arriving at the Afton St footbridge to cross the river.

 RIGHT HERE marks the exact spot that divides the day's ride into two halves as you move from inner-urban area to more rural landscapes.

Check if your tyres need pumping and fill up your water bottle before proceeding, but not before a dose of forest bathing as you make a quick detour to check out the **Afton Street Conservation Reserve**, with a boardwalk overlooking biodiverse wetlands. Then it's up and around for what's a steep, kilojoule-burning climb that's well worth all the huffing and puffing for the sublime views awaiting you over this sweeping river bend, with the city skyline as a backdrop. Here you'll also spot the sprawling **Maribyrnong Defence Site**, a historic military area used for many years as both an explosives factory (including where .303 bullets used in Gallipoli and the Somme were manufactured) and a testing site right up until the 1990s. Today it's totally abandoned, and though it's been up for sale, contaminated soils may prevent developers coming in anytime soon.

 AFTER FINALLY CATCHING YOUR BREATH, you'll fly down the path to turn left just before the underpass to join the downhill dirt trail over the confluence of the Maribyrnong and Stele Creek. And right about here is where you'll have that 'where the hell am I?' moment as you find yourself among some remote and arid bushland. But don't worry; the river's not far off and when you do reunite, it'll barely be recognisable as you're spat out at a pristine stretch of river red gums with no infrastructure in sight.

➥ **FROM HERE** you'll bump along the dirt track for the remainder of the ride as you make your way through Avondale Heights's native grassland reserves and parks. And when they say you never know what lies around the next corner, this is a good example, as the biggest Vietnamese Buddhist temple outside Vietnam, **Quang Minh Buddhist Temple** (`quangminh.org.au`), appears on a hilltop among the Australian bush where its Laughing Buddha sits.

➥ **NOT FAR FROM HERE,** keep an eye out for the (unsigned) rock crossing of **Solomon's Ford**; one of the river's several basalt weirs where Wurundjeri and Bunurong Peoples would catch eels using woven funnel traps and cross to the other side, something local walkers still do to get back and forth to other side in Sunshine.

Thompson Reserve is the last opportunity to fill up your bottle as you make your way along the Maribyrnong's scenic natural course while keeping your eyes peeled for the red rump parrot, superb blue wrens and the peregrine falcon hunting from above.

➥ **THE NEXT STOP** is a beauty: the imposing **Maribyrnong River Viaduct**, a historic rail trestle bridge that stretches 383m across the bush-filled gully. It's Victoria's second tallest bridge, a mere 3m less than the West Gate, and despite being built in 1929, it's still used by freight trains – it'll have you feeling as if you've arrived on location in *Stand By Me*. Soon it will have company, as this is the site of Melbourne's new airport rail bridge that'll one day go up alongside this heritage-listed structure – or so they've said every election year for the past few decades!

➥ **AHEAD** stands another soaring landmark, the **EJ Whitten Bridge**, named after an equally big presence in the area: Teddy Whitten, VFL football legend and Footscray's most famous son.

➲ **AT THIS POINT** no doubt you're feeling it, but dig in deep for the final 2.5km to reach the finishing point (or halfway mark, anyway) where you'll be rewarded with a long, leisurely lunch break at **Brimbank Park**. The stylish **Lumbar & Co** (instagram.com/lumbar.co) is a welcome sight in the middle of the park with outdoor seating for you to enjoy quality cafe fare and drinks while looking out to the park.

Parks Victoria manages Brimbank Park and at the cafe you'll find the visitor centre with a rundown on things to see and do, including early European remnants, such as the 1860s Dodd Homestead or the Horseshoe Bend farm with its original cottages. The park was settled by Europeans in the 1830s, where it was named after farmers moving their livestock 'around the brim of the bank' of the Maribyrnong. But well before then, the Wurundjeri People resided here. Nearby was the famous 1940 archaeological discovery of the **Keilor Cranium**. This, and other finds in the area, have been carbon dated to 31,000 years ago – so right where you stand is one of the oldest sites of human habitation in Australia. Also found here were megafauna remains of thylacoleo (marsupial lion) and diprotodont, a 2m-tall wombat! While you're not likely to spot anything that impressive these days, if you're lucky you can see swamp wallabies, blue-tongue lizards and echidnas, as well as brush-tailed and ringtail possums residing in the river red gums.

⚑ **ONCE YOU'RE RESTED, REHYDRATED AND REJUVENATED**, it's time to get back on the bike for the return ride. Don't worry: without all the stops it's a much quicker trip. Finish off at Footscray's **Inner West Bike Hub** (communitybikehub.com.au) for a post-ride service, and hang out while you grab a pizza and drink from its attached **Lickety Split** (fourpeople.com.au) cafe, and its cool laneway complex, before jumping back on the train home.

Local Chit-chat with Tony Cavallaro

Co-owner of T Cavallaro & Sons Pasticceria
(tcavallaroandsons.com.au; 98 Hopkins St, Footscray;
8.30am–4pm Tue to Fri, 8am–3pm Sat, 9am–noon Sun)

When did the cafe open?

My parents, Tommaso and Sarina, came out to Australia in 1949
from Lipari, Sicily, and opened Pasticceria in 1956 with the
help of my eldest brother Carmelo – who has only just recently
retired. I was only three months old at the time, however. And
while I often helped out on weekends as a kid growing up,
I didn't start work there till I left school.

What were your early impressions of life in Footscray back then?

My early impressions of Footscray were my formative ones.
I took my first steps in the shop; we went to school there in the
area; made lifelong friends; played football with a Footscray
jumper for St Monica's. On Saturday nights we went to the local
Italian cinema as a family.

How do you see Footscray today?

I see Footscray now very much as I saw it then, a place where
people settle to raise a family, even though many singles and
couples are now settling into apartments because of our
proximity to the CBD. But Footscray has always been a melting
pot of different cultures and with that, different foods.

How has your cafe changed over the years? Is it still family owned?

Our bakery hasn't changed much; when we talk of change to our customers, they invariably tell us not to change a thing, that its appeal is in its '60s look. It is still family-owned by my wife Rosa and myself with my son Robert being the next generation.

What are the specialities that you recommend visitors try?

What we are best known for is our cannoli, either ricotta or patisserie-cream filled. Our traditional Sicilian biscotti, pastini di mandorla and amaretti are also a must and the recipe has not changed since our grandfather.

CLICK, READ, LISTEN AND WATCH:

- footscrayhistoricalsociety.org.au
- Rick Kea, *Keilor to Footscray: Mr Solomon's Maribyrnong*
- Camp Cope, 'Footscray Station'
  Scott & Charlene's Wedding, 'Footscray Station'
- *Palazzo Di Cozzo* (2021, directed by Madeleine Martiniello)
  Year of the Dogs (1997, directed by Michael Cordell & Stewart Young)

MERRI CREEK TRAIL

WESTERN
RING ROAD
THOMASTOWN

GOWRIE
STATION

Bababi
Djinanang

FAWKNER

RESERVOIR

Coburg
drive-in
cinema

ISLAMIC MUSEUM AUSTRALIA

Coburg
Lake
Reserve

HM
Prison
Pentridge

COBURG

Joe's
Market
Garden

Islamic
Museum
of
Australia

Moreland Road

Brunswick
Velodrome

CERES

BRUNSWICK
EAST

Merri
Creek
Reserve

NORTHCOTE

FITZROY
NORTH

DIGHTS
FALLS

START
Western Ring Rd, Thomastown

FINISH
Dights Falls, Abbotsford

DISTANCE
19km one-way

DURATION
3-6 hours return

TRANSPORT
Take the Upfield line to Gowrie station from where it's a 2km ride to the trailhead of the Merri Creek Trail, just south of Mahoneys Rd in Thomastown. If driving, park in the backstreets where the Western Ring Path joins up with Merri Creek.

CONNECTING RIDES

Capital City Trail (p28)

Main Yarra Trail

St Georges Rd Bike Path

Western Ring Road Trail

Snaking its way through Merri Creek's enchanting landscapes is this trail that delights with a mix of nature-filled sanctuaries, varied local history, multicultural landmarks and community-driven attractions that'll leave you astounded at the variety you can pack into a half-day's ride.

WHILE 'THOMASTOWN' AND 'TOURIST DESTINATION' are two things you're not likely to hear in the same sentence, this is where things kick off for what is arguably Melbourne's most scenic bike trail. Along with Fawkner and Reservoir, it's good to see some of the lesser-visited northern suburbs represented as you take off along beautiful Merri Creek's slender course, a trail that follows the lower reaches of the creek's journey – one that starts 50km north in the foothills of the Great Dividing Range near Heathcote Junction.

⚐ CYCLING WITH KIDS: Kids can come prepped with a checklist of birds and wildlife to tick off as you zip past bushland mixed with parks and lakes. They will love **CERES**, not just for lunch stop but also the chickens and a popular sandpit filled with Tonka trucks. The many informative signage boards make this one of Melbourne's most educational rides as well.

● **THE BEAUTY OF THESE DEDICATED BIKE TRAILS** is that they lead you off the main roads and into a whole new world, so while the Western Ring Rd may not sound like the most appealing place to start a nature ride, don't worry: you'll be leaving it behind in your dust as you take the dirt track to be immersed among Merri Creek's bushland wilderness. Lined with water reeds, river gums and rocky grasslands, this secluded part of the park is home not just to abundant birdlife but also to native animals you don't often associate with Melbourne, like swamp wallabies, snakes and blue-tongue lizards, the odd waddling echidna, and even platypus among other species. This is the land of the Wurundjeri People, the Traditional Custodians of the Merri Merri, a word that translates as 'very rocky creek'.

● **AS YOU REACH** a small bridge that leads over the creek keep on going straight, which brings you to the golden rule of the ride: if signs go missing, just so long as you can still see the creek you're going the right way!

● **AS THE PATH TURNS TO BITUMEN,** the landscape opens right up as you ride through the grasslands of **Bababi Djinanang**, a 4ha reserve home to 70-plus species of native plants and where eastern grey kangaroos are occasionally spotted transiting through. And though it's an area fringed by residential development, enjoy the peacefulness of life out here as you glide by arid rocky gullies dotted with prickly pear – a local scourge, we should mention – reminiscent of a Mexican landscape.

● **YOU'LL PASS** by the back of **Coburg drive-in cinema**, the largest in the Southern Hemisphere, a remnant from the good ol' days dating to 1965, before you cross a footbridge that brings you into **Coburg Lake Reserve.** This is where Merri Creek's course takes a dramatic shift as it balloons into a picturesque English-style lake garden complete with weeping willows, ducks and swans. Here the path leads up past the lake by a cool playground that features a giant outdoor game of Twister, before passing the *Man of the Valley* sculpture who stands overlooking a cliff face that's a cutting from the park's historical bluestone quarry.

From here you'll ride down to 'Bin Chicken Island', a sanctuary for the much-maligned (and unfairly, in our opinion) Australian white ibis.

⊙ **WHEN YOU REACH THE BRIDGE** at the weir's cascading falls, there's s an optional 500m detour to check out one of Coburg's most infamous landmarks – **HM Prison Pentridge.** It was a prison so notorious that the suburb of Coburg was actually once called Pentridge before it changed its name in 1870 to avoid association with this terrifying bluestone clinker! (It's not only the time Coburg's been involved in a name change, with Moreland City Council announcing in late 2021 it plans to change its name to avoid a historical association to a Jamaican sugar plantation owner.)

While Pentridge has since taken on a whole new life – having been redeveloped into luxury apartments, a cinema and an arts hub after its closure in 1997 – its heritage listing means its formidable structure and the main gate tower remain as petrifying as ever. Incidentally, some of the bluestone bricks used to build it were sourced from this park's very site.

But if you don't want to go to Pentridge – and who can blame you? – stick to the trail to pass the fish ladder: a water passage built to assist common galaxia and short-finned eel in their journey along the creek. If you think a 19km bike ride is far, spare a thought for the short-finned eel who one day will embark on an epic 5000-km journey from freshwater to the Coral Sea (between New Caledonia and Papua New Guinea) to spawn.

⊙ **LEAVE THE PARK** via the bridge and turn right at the basketball arena where you'll find yourself back on the Merri Creek Trail. Disappear beneath the bluestone Murray Rd Bridge before stopping ahead to read up on the life and culture of the Wurundjeri People that's detailed along this stretch. You'll then cross another bridge to land back on the other side of the creek as you fly through parkland and

Joe's Market Garden (ceres.org.au/farm-food/joes-market-garden/), an organic veggie patch on just under a hectare that's been farmed by Chinese and Italian gardeners for over 150 years. As well picking up some homegrown produce, you can stop in for a coffee before wheeling over Harding St Bridge to arrive in **Preston** and **Thornbury**, where Melbourne's cool kids now hang out after being priced out of their old inner-north stomping ground, a shift Courtney Barnett sings about on her track 'Depreston'.

⮕ **YOU'LL ONLY SKIRT THROUGH** these suburbs' parkland and reserves before reaching a T-intersection at busy Moreland Rd, where there's an opportunity for a cultural detour to visit the **Islamic Museum of Australia** (islamicmuseum.org.au) to learn of Australia's Muslim history from 'Afghan' cameleers and Malay Pearlers to Islamic art displays and themed exhibitions.

⮕ **RETURN BACK** to Moreland Rd via Anderson Rd where you'll cross over carefully and take a right before turning down Clara St to meet up with the **East Brunswick** section of the trail. At **Merri Corner Community Garden** (merricorner.org) you'll notice a mural of the sacred kingfisher, a beautiful bird with striking turquoise plumage that's symbolic of the creek's change in fortunes. Like many Melburnians, this bird likes to spend its winters up north in sunny Queensland, but when Merri Creek was turned into a rubbish tip and industrial dumping ground in the 1970s, it didn't return for decades. But thanks to all the hard work by local environmentalists, it was sighted again in 1993 – leading to the annual Return of the Sacred Kingfisher Festival – and today remains a regular visitor to the creek.

⮕ **STOP TO TAKE A LOOK** at speeding cyclists circling around **Brunswick Velodrome**, and possibly sneak in a quick lap, just because you can, before coming across the unexpected sight of the gleaming golden onion baubles of **Pokrov Russian Orthodox Cathedral** (pokrov.com.au), another shining example of multicultural Brunswick.

⊖ **REACHING THE HALFWAY MARK,** you'll be pleased to hear the next stop is for lunch, and a memorable one at that, as you pull into **CERES** (`ceres.org.au`). Named as both an acronym (Centre for Education and Research in Environmental Strategies) and after the Roman goddess of agriculture, Ceres, this social enterprise was established back in 1982 and today remains a much-loved part of the Brunswick East community for its efforts in promoting everything environmental, conservation and sustainable – from permaculture to organic farming. Pop in to the visitor centre to get the lowdown on the place before grabbing anything from vegan sausage rolls to free-range organic lunches, along with a choice of local craft beers and wines.

⊖ **REPLENISHED AND REFUELLED,** get back on the bike because it's time to pedal on as you're treated to one of the most pleasing legs of the trail passing through Northcote's bushy Merri Creek Reserve, a shaggy wilderness that leads on to scenic willow-lined banks. Further up is a steep climb looping around North Fitzroy's St Georges Rd that leads over the bridge where a bike repair station awaits for any mid-trail adjustments. The trail runs along Merri Pde before crossing back over the creek via a footbridge to join forces with the **Capital City Trail** (p28) as it passes beneath Rushall station's underpass to loop around back to the creek. (An alternative is via a quiet backstreet sojourn along Cunningham St to turn right at McLachlan to meet another footbridge leading over the creek).

It's right around this bushy section of Merri Creek that many believe is the site where on 6 June 1835, John Batman met with Wurundjeri Elders to sign what became known as **Batman's treaty.** In exchange for blankets, handkerchiefs, mirrors, clothing, tomahawks, knives and 68kg (150lb) of flour, it was a deal that landed Batman some 243,000ha of land that now comprises Melbourne. If that seems like a steal, it's because it was!

⚑ **AHEAD** lie some natural wetlands and shaded bends as you wind through Fairfield, Clifton Hill and then on to Abbotsford to reach the finish line at Dights Falls. It's here where Merri Creek finishes its journey to join forces with the Yarra River, an event that takes place in what is one Melbourne's most scenic viewpoints. It's a confluence that was both an important river crossing for the Wurundjeri People as well a meeting and trading place with other tribes of the Kulin Nation, and is believed to be the burial place of clan Elder Billibellary, one of the eight Wurundjeri individuals present during the signing of the Batman Treaty. It makes it a fitting place to reflect on Melbourne's ancient past, the present and unknown next chapters of its future that lie ahead. It's then back on the bike for either what will be return leg, a 1km ride to Victoria Park station, or, riding further along the Yarra via the **Capital City Trail** (p28).

Local Chit-chat with Ann McGregor

Ann McGregor and her husband, Bruce, are local environmentalists and long-time campaigners for the protection and restoration of Merri Creek. Ann is both president of Merri Creek Management Committee (mcmc.org.au) and vice president of Friends of Merri Creek (friendsofmerricreek.org.au)

How long have you and your husband Bruce been involved with the clean-up of Merri Creek and how did it all come about?

We went on a walk along the Merri in East Brunswick in 1976, organised by Brunswick Community Group. From that a Brunswick Merri Creek Action Group was formed, and we were active members. From there it was a logical step to help establish the Merri Creek Coordinating Committee, then Friends of Merri Creek and Merri Creek Management Committee.

You guys helped set up Friends of Merri Creek, so please tell us briefly about that. And what's the best way for people to help out in keeping the creek healthy and clean?

We were among the founders of Friends of Merri Creek, which was formed from quite a number of local groups in 1988. The Friends have been active in planting, weeding, litter collection, water-quality monitoring, campaigns and advocacy to protect the creek corridor from threats (including a freeway), community information, and being part of the Merri Creek Management Committee. People can help keep the creek healthy by picking up after their dog, not littering in streets (because streets drain to creeks), and getting involved in community events along the Merri.

Do you have some personal favourite sections along the Merri Creek Trail?

The section between Blyth Street and Moreland Road, East Brunswick is probably our favourite – closest to home and where we lead bird surveys four times a year.

Any tips for best enjoying the area?

Take your time. Coburg Lake Reserve and Kirkdale Park (just downstream of Victoria Street, East Brunswick) are good places for a picnic or barbecue. The Islamic Museum cafe has tasty, simple meals and drinks and has an entrance from the Merri Trail, upstream of Normanby Road.

What kinds of wildlife can people be lucky enough to see?

Occasionally a swamp wallaby spends some time along the Merri corridor. There are eels and turtles in the creek, and a rakali (native water rat, with a white-tipped tail) lives in Coburg Lake. There are blue-tongue lizards and several species of snakes, too.

How about birdlife?

The Friends of Merri Creek bird surveys at 10 sites between
Clifton Hill and Craigieburn have recorded over 140 species.
Sharp-eyed observers can find tawny frogmouths roosting in
trees along the trail. Many bush birds like spotted pardalotes
and grey fantails have returned to the Merri corridor since
revegetation began in the 1980s. Ducks, moorhens and
cormorants are reasonably common in the creek. Towards the
edge of the northern suburbs, grassland birds and raptors can
be seen. Reed warblers and sacred kingfishers are among the
migratory birds that return to the Merri in spring to breed.

CLICK, READ, LISTEN AND WATCH:

🌐 friendsofmerricreek.org.au
  mcmc.org.au

📖 Don Osborne, *Pentridge – Behind the Bluestone Walls*
  Ian D Clark and Toby Heydon, *Bend in the Yarra: A History of
    the Merri Creek*

🎵 Not Drowning, Waving, 'Thomastown'

BELGRAVE RAIL TRAIL

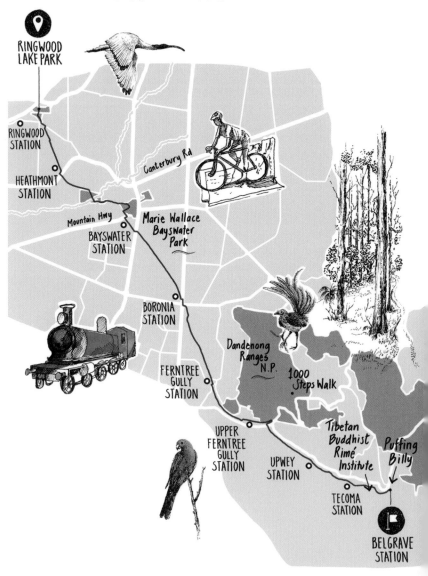

RINGWOOD LAKE PARK

RINGWOOD STATION

HEATHMONT STATION

Mountain Hwy

Canterbury Rd

BAYSWATER STATION

Marie Wallace Bayswater Park

BORONIA STATION

FERNTREE GULLY STATION

Dandenong Ranges N.P.

1000 Steps Walk

UPPER FERNTREE GULLY STATION

UPWEY STATION

Tibetan Buddhist Rimé Institute

Puffing Billy

TECOMA STATION

BELGRAVE STATION

START
Ringwood Lake Park

FINISH
Belgrave

DISTANCE
19km one-way

DURATION
4–6 hours return

TRANSPORT
Ringwood Lake Park is a
five-minute ride from
the station, or otherwise
there's plenty of parking at
the lake. To return you can
ride back, or take the train
from Belgrave.

CONNECTING RIDES
Dandenong Creek Trail

EastLink Trail

Ferny Creek Trail

Taralla Creek Trail

Representing the eastern suburbs is this rollicking
railway-themed ride that runs alongside the
passenger line from Ringwood to Belgrave.
Taking you through some of Melbourne's lesser-
visited suburbs, this dedicated bike trail
leads among parks and bushland of the Dandenong
Ranges National Park before arriving for a fun,
nostalgic-filled train journey as you hop aboard
the beloved *Puffing Billy* steam train.

CELEBRATED IN EVERYTHING from *Kath & Kim* and *Neighbours* to the *Castle* and Howard Arkley's paintings, Melbourne's 'burbs are a much loved part of the city, not only for their daggy familiarity but also for their unsung cultural contribution to what truly makes this city tick. And nowhere better represents the outer suburbs than good ol' Ringwood, the beginning of today's ride, 30km from the city centre in Melbourne's outer east.

CYCLING WITH KIDS: Puffing Billy should definitely be part of the plan, so don't set off too late. At **Marie Wallace Park** kids can zip around the bike school for a crash-course in road safety – not literally, of course! Then take in **war museums** and **Tibetan monasteries** before you hop on **Puffing Billy.**

● **EASTLAND** may be what many most associate with Ringwood, but thankfully we're starting off somewhere a bit more scenic than a shopping centre: **Ringwood Lake Park**, a beautiful reserve sanctuary; it's worth packing a picnic for the trip out here alone. As well as picturesque bird-filled wetlands, there's a small open-air museum detailing Ringwood's 19th-century antimony mining industry – a mineral *Forbes* magazine describes as 'the most important mineral you never heard of'. It's vital for powering iPhones and all military high-tech needs, so who knows, maybe one day again we'll see this rusty old mining equipment dusted off and cranked back into gear! And that's not the only semiprecious natural resource found out this way. If you're a beer lover, you'll be interested to know that just up the road from here is where the Pride of Ringwood was grown, a type of hops used in many of Australia's most famous beers, from VB to Foster's Lager.

But that's enough titbits of info for now; it's time to get on with the ride. Though just before you do, a heads-up that this is a trail that at times can feel a little disjointed, so you can expect any number of cut-throughs, switchbacks and detours as you take a route that links up three different bike trails. Don't worry: it's all pretty easy, and just as long as you're within the vicinity of the train line, you're going the right way.

➲ **STARTING OUT** from the southern part of the lake, look out for the sign pointing to the Heathmont Rail Trail. This is where you'll exit the park to cross over at the boom gates to ride by the community centre and turn left along Rosewarne Lane. At Bedford Rd take another left to pass Ringwood Secondary School before crossing over at the lights to dart down Lena Grove. This is the official starting point for the **Heathmont Rail Trail** where the leafy bike path follows alongside the train tracks of the Belgrave line that runs from the city into Belgrave. Here you'll fly through the suburb of Heathmont, where houses were once fruit orchards, before reaching Heathmont station, where the trail takes a brief interlude to cross the intersection at Canterbury Rd with its busy shopping strip including **Milk + Wine Co.** (milkandwine.com.au) if you're looking for a decent coffee. From the station, take a right to head along the shared pavement to cross at the pedestrian lights where the path continues along the train line for a glorious freewheelin' downhill stretch. At the sports reserve we momentarily say goodbye to the train line as you wind past the basketball arena to cross a small bridge that leads over the confluence where Dandenong and Bungalook creeks meet.

This is where we pay our respects to the Bunurong People, the Traditional Owners past and present, where for thousands of years (right up until European settlement) a permanent camp existed right here that was a rich hunting ground for kangaroos, possum, geese, swan, fish and eel.

⊙ **CROSSING THE BRIDGE** you'll take a left to link up with the **Dandenong Creek Trail** for a short scenic leg running alongside this urban creek that travels 53km from the Dandenong Ranges to the Patterson River, from where it flows into Port Phillip Bay/Nerm at Carrum.

⊙ **ALONG THIS STRETCH** keep an eye out for the monument dedicated to 'Oppy': the legendary Australian cyclist, **Sir Hubert Ferdinand Opperman** (1904–96). It's one of five statues found along the three adjoining trails known as the 'Oppy Route' (`knox.vic.gov.au/our-services/sports-parks-playgrounds-and-reserves/sports-and-leisure/cycling`) to commemorate one of Australia's sporting heroes, who, alongside Bradman and Phar Lap, was revered during the Depression-era 1930s, smashing endurance records worldwide on his locally built Malvern Star bike. Post-riding career he moved into federal politics as Minister of Immigration before becoming Australia's first High Commissioner to Malta, but he rode till the very end, literally: passing away on his exercise bike one month short of turning of 91!

⊙ **AFTER ABOUT 2KM** you'll leave the Dandenong Creek Trail to join the beginning of the **Belgrave Rail Trail**, where you'll take a right to arrive at **Marie Wallace Bayswater Park**. Named after the first female mayor of the Knox City Council, it's better known as the 'train park', one where generations of kids have scrambled aboard the resplendent red 120-year-old red steam engine; a D3 class 4-6-0 for all the trainspotters out there. The park also makes a good spot for a toilet stop, to refill your water and pump up the tyres at the bike repair station. Plus there's also a fun little bike school for kids to learn the road rules when they're done playing on the train.

⊘ **NEXT,** cut through the south-west of the park to reach King St, which leads on to the Mountain Hwy in the suburb of Bayswater. At the highway, take a right to follow the shared pedestrian–cyclist footpath past an understated white-brick Hindu temple. The trail loops up and around to do a U-turn leading you beneath the underpass to arrive at Bayswater train station. If you feel it's easier to start your ride here rather than Ringwood, this is a good option to begin or end the trail if you're after a more abridged version of the ride.

⊘ **HERE** the bike trail will shoot you through onto Scoresby Rd where you'll cross over to continue along Power Rd through Bayswater's commercial estate. It's not overly pretty out here, but the Dandenong foothills looming in the distance serve as a lure to the charms of what lies ahead. But among these industrial backstreets is a hidden gem in **Hard Road Brewing** (hardroadbrewing.com), which appears from this gritty area like a mirage for any thirsty passer-by. Run by an American husband–wife team, this taphouse is set in a warehouse among their brewery tanks where you can sample an interesting selection of craft ales along with guest breweries. To get here, ride up Woodmason Rd and turn left at Freedman Ave before cutting through the park; call ahead first to check they're open.

⊘ **BACK ON THE TRAIL,** continue along this long stretch by the train tracks till you reach Boronia station where a monstrosity of a shopping centre awaits. Admittedly, having to navigate through here is not the highlight of the day's ride; first make your way through its car park before crossing over the heaving 10-lane intersection nightmare that is Boronia Rd. But as a sweetener to soften the blow, there's plenty of excellent multicultural food out this way. And if you need any accessories or mid-ride tune-ups, then **Mac's Cycles** (maccycles.com.au) is here for you.

Once you clear the mess, head left along Maryville Way, passing the Boronia Hotel to get back on track along the rail trail through Boronia's gum tree–filled streets as you stick to the train line.

● **FROM THIS POINT** the ride becomes progressively more scenic as you reach Ferntree Gully and its forested backdrop of the Dandenong Ranges; a word derived from Tangeong, meaning 'mountain' and 'creek' in the Bunurong language. Suddenly the air feels fresher as you cycle through the carpark of Ferntree Gully station before turning right at Alpine St to cross over the tracks and on to the other side of the road. The trail continues along the train line where the *Belgrave Express* flies by to the same destination you're heading. You'll then pedal up and over an old steel-caged bridge before coasting down a winding downhill section that brings you beside the Burwood Hwy, where a sign officially 'Welcomes you to the Dandenong Ranges'. With its lush fern-filled eucalypt forests and charming villages with ye olde taverns and teahouses, it's an area that's been attracting holiday-makers as a quaint getaway for more than 150 years.

● **THE NEXT SUBURB ALONG** is Upper Ferntree Gully, and seeing all these houses set on bush blocks, even the most pretentious of black-clad inner-city snobs may concede living the 'Australian dream' out here in the sticks seems pretty damn appealing right now

● **AT THE TRAIN STATION,** turn left into Railway Ave to cross at the boom gates and continue alongside the Belgrave line; before you know it you're in the **Dandenong Ranges National Park** (`parks.vic.gov.au/places-to-see/parks/dandenong-ranges-national-park`). That's right, Melbourne has a national park! What doesn't this city have?

You'll find yourself briefly on a dirt track that skirts this tranquil tract of forest with giant mountain ash and tree ferns that wallabies, wombats and lyrebirds call home. The trail passes a back-route entry to the **1000 Steps Walk**, long a popular hike among Melburnians, particularly for fitness fanatics who come here to pound the steps in the latest activewear. It's a walk dedicated to the Australian soldiers who endured the gruelling Kokoda Trail in Papua New Guinea in World War II. But don't worry; given you're on a bike ride, we're not going suggest you walk this too. But come back to visit on another day as it's a wonderful spot for a leisurely bushwalk, while taking in a dose of forest bathing and birdwatching.

⊙ **AFTER THIS BRIEF RIDE** through the national park, the bike path rejoins the Burwood Hwy where you'll cross over two sets of lights to double back and loop around where the track rejoins the train line. Along this stretch you'll see a profusion of birdlife, catching glimpses of vivid plumage as rosellas and king parrots flit about while kookaburra laughs merrily from the ol' gum tree.

If you're like us, by this point you've cycled up quite a thirst, especially given this bit's quite a slog, so you may be wondering where's the next water stop. The answer to that it that there's basically none! So when you reach Upwey where the bike trail loops around again to the Burwood Hwy, a stop at 7-Eleven may be on the cards. But aside from a Slurpee, another reason to cross over the road here is to check out the **Running Rabbits Military Museum** (upweybelgraversl.org.au/museum). Set up by the Upwey Belgrave RSL, the museum covers Australia's entire military history, from the Boer War and the two world wars to the current day. But the focus of the museum is the Kokoda campaign, in keeping with the nearby Kokoka 1000 Steps walking trail with its 12 memorial plaques. It's a fascinating collection with ever-changing exhibits, and out front you'll find a Leopard tank and anti-submarine Ikara missile. There's also a bistro here at what is one of the few RSLs not to have pokies. As to what the 'running rabbits' meaning is all about, that's a reference to a controversial speech by General Thomas Blamey (aka 'that bastard Blamey') who caused outrage among soldiers expecting to be praised for holding off the Japanese only to be accused off running like rabbits.

⊜ **FROM 7-ELEVEN,** the trail runs alongside the road for a downhill section to pass Upwey station before swinging around to meet Main St and then back again by the Burwood Hwy. It's a gradual uphill push before reaching Glenfern Rd to get off the highway, but it's not long before you're making another infuriating detour at Tecoma station. Follow Campbell St to turn right on to McNichol Rd, and turn left to meet the trail again for the final leg; it's a beautiful section through a valley of tree ferns to a soundtrack of nature. After about 300m, keep an eye out for Dickinson St where you can pedal off the trail for a short ride to take a look at the **Tibetan Buddhist Rimé Institute** (`rimebuddhism.com`). Though not quite the Potala, rather a weatherboard draped in prayer flags, it was founded by Tibetan monk Khentrul Rinpoche (`khentrulrinpoche.com/about`) in 2005.

⊜ **NEXT** you'll reach the finishing post as you pull into Belgrave train station, so congratulations on your arrival. But, of course, this is not really the end of the line, and in fact it's the just beginning of a whole new adventure as it's all aboard Puffing Billy! Dating back to 1900, **Puffing Billy** (`puffingbilly.com.au`) is a restored steam locomotive used as a passenger and cargo service from Belgrave to Gembrook until it was discontinued in the 1950s. But the train was so well loved that enthusiasts kept it going as a scenic tourist train, and 70-odd years on here we are. You're not a true Melburnian until you've dangled your legs over the window sill on this scenic train journey, one of many quirky little rituals this city loves across generations.

Puffing Billy's departure makes for a dramatic scene as it builds up a head of steam at its Belgrave station to take off in cloud of smoke while sounding the whistle to chug its way through the fern gullies of Dandenong Ranges. There are a few journeys available (check the website) but most make the trip over the iconic Monbulk Creek trestle bridge and through Sherbrooke Forest to the charming township of Gembrook. And before you set off on the ride, bear in mind the last journey is at 12.30pm, so you'll want to get pedalling before 9am to make sure you're here in time.

⚑ **IF YOU'RE NOT HERE FOR PUFFING BILLY,** Belgrave is well worthy of exploration. Ride along the graffiti-splattered Blacksmith Way and carry your bike up the stairs to explore the village-like main strip with a bohemian feel and local characters (most famously the Wizard of Belgrave). As you wheel your bike along, check out the cafes and restaurants. If you're here on the second Sunday of the month, you can also check out **Big Dreams Market** (`belgravebigdreamsmarket.com`) with buskers, food and art-and-craft stalls. And if you want to make a night of it, drop in to **Sooki Lounge** (`sookilounge.com.au`) with live music, dinner and drinks before taking the last train back to Melbourne. But more than likely you're here purely for the riding, in which case it's a matter of retracing your tread to make your way back along the trail as you race the train back to Flinders St.

Local Chit-chat with Belinda McKenzie

Belinda McKenzie is a steam train enthusiast and Puffing Billy driver.

It must've been an honour to be the first female driver of Puffing Billy in 120-plus years of its history? How was that experience?

Being selected as a trainee driver and learning how to drive the wonderful Puffing Billy steam trains was a unique and rewarding experience. The locomotives are intricate machines that are lovingly repaired and maintained as close to their original early 1900s form as possible. Stepping into the running shed on a crisp winter morning to greet the firemen who have been gently tending their fires and building steam for the coming day, the engine cleaners who have been polishing the brass and paintwork since before the sun was up, and the other drivers is like stepping into another world. We put away our electronic devices and the trappings of the modern world, share a cuppa, and enjoy bringing to life our little part of the living museum that is Puffing Billy.

How did you come about working for Puffing Billy, and what's your advice to others wanting to get involved as volunteers?

I started volunteering for Puffing Billy in late 2010 after taking a ride as a passenger and being invited to have a look inside the engine by that day's crew. I loved what I saw and asked the crew about how they came to be there, after which I learned that they were volunteers. It all just snowballed from there. There are so many roles at the railway. Just in case black fingers aren't your thing, most roles are not as dirty as the engineman's pathway, which starts as an engine cleaner. Also, you don't have to know what you want from the beginning. Once you start as a volunteer, you may discover a role you never knew existed that just lights a spark inside you. My advice to anyone who wants to get involved as a volunteer is to give it a try. You never know where it will end up.

What are some of your favourite things to do around the Dandenong Ranges?

I love nature, so taking walks around the hills is something I try to do when I have time. There are plenty of trails to be found for both walkers and cyclists, including the new mixed-use trail that runs alongside the Puffing Billy track. A special highlight of that track is that it runs along the railway for much of the very steep 1:30 grade between Cockatoo and Gembrook that we refer to as Fielder Bank. That is the steepest part of the line and a real challenge for locomotive crews. The train typically slows to around 7 miles per hour (about 11km per hour for those with metric minds), meaning very fit cyclists may be able to keep up with and pace the train for a bit.

The Dandenong Ranges is a big area with so much on offer, but some of my favourite spots further afield would include Emerald Lake Park, especially in autumn when it turns a vibrant mix of autumn colours; One Tree Hill and its associated trails; the daffodil fields near Hermons Corner and, of course, the many cute places you can stop to get afternoon tea.

CLICK, READ, LISTEN AND WATCH:

- bunuronglc.org
- Daniel Oakman, *Oppy: The Life of Sir Hubert Opperman*, David Burke (ed.), *Saving Puffing Billy*
- Slim Dusty, 'Kokoda Track'
- *Kokoda* (2006, directed by Alister Grierson)

NEIGHBOURHOOD

JAUNTS

A RIDE TO RICHMOND

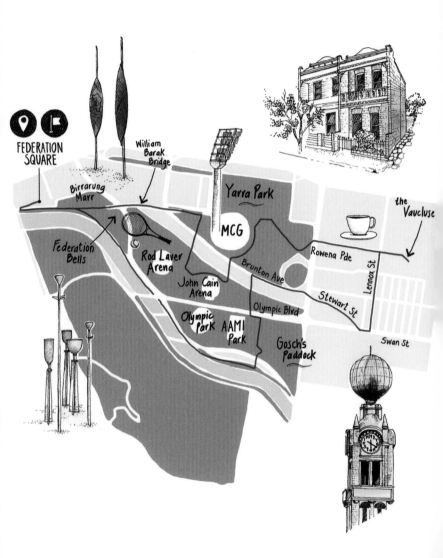

FEDERATION SQUARE

Birrarung Marr

William Barak Bridge

Federation Bells

Rod Laver Arena

John Cain Arena

Olympic Park

AAMI Park

Yarra Park

MCG

Brunton Ave

Olympic Blvd

Gosch's Paddock

Rowena Pde

Stewart St

Lennox St

Swan St

the Vaucluse

START // FINISH
Federation Square

 DISTANCE
10km loop

 DURATION
half- to full-day

TRANSPORT
Flinders Street Station or
Richmond Station

 CONNECTING RIDES
**Capital City Trail
(p28)**
Main Yarra Trail

If Melbourne's the sporting capital of the world
(a city so sporting mad it has a public holiday
not just for a horse race, but also for the AFL
Grand Final) then Richmond is its epicentre. This
bike trail connects some of the city's most famous
sporting landmarks as it takes in Richmond's local
history, culture and food stops to suit all tastes.

IT'S TAKEN THE BEST PART of 20 years, but finally Melburnians have embraced the ugly duckling that is **Federation Square** (`fedsquare.com`) as the gathering and cultural place it was intended to be. Voted by the UK's *Daily Telegraph* as the world's eighth ugliest building of the 21st century, if you think this misunderstood landmark is an eyesore, you should've seen what it was beforehand! First the site of a 19th-century morgue, and, more recently, soulless 1960s office blocks that many argued were just as grim.

🚴 **CYCLING WITH KIDS:** Start at **Federation Square** where there's no shortage of stuff to do, but be sure to make time for the **Koorie Heritage Trust** – an educational first stop. At **Birrarung Marr**, you'll find **ArtPlay**, with a regular roster of children's activities that you need to pre-book. The **Federation Bells** will intrigue before you cross the 'singing bridge'. At **Melbourne Park**, check to see if Australian Open tours are running again, or have a hit on one of its courts through **Tennis World** (`tennisworld.net.au`). At the mighty **MCG** book a tour for a behind-the-scenes look, before heading into the Australian Sports Museum to learn about our sporting greats and test your skills at anything from kicking a footy and shooting hoops to classic catches. On into Richmond proper, where there are plenty of choices for food and drink before the scenic ride back.

● **IT'S HERE** at Fed Square you'll kick things off, where among its many cultural attractions and festivities you'll find the **Koorie Heritage Trust** (kooorieheritagetrust.com.au). It makes a fitting first stop, not just to pay your respects to the Traditional Owners, the Woiwurrung (Wurundjeri) People – who've lived by the banks of the Yarra for many thousands of years – but to learn of the cultures of the peoples across the entire Kulin Nation. And if you're around at 1pm Wednesday to Friday, don't miss the fascinating one-hour guided tours that take place along **Birrarung Marr.**

If you can't make the tour, no stress, as this is the next stop regardless as you roll down to arrive at the three-terraced riverside park precinct. Translating loosely as 'River of Mists' ('Birrarung' being the Wurundjeri name for the Yarra and 'Marr' meaning mist) here you'll pass a series of open-air art installations known collectively as **Birrarung Wilam.** Among the interpretive panels are a winding textured carved eel pathway, scarred message sticks, the five metal shields and spears representing five tribes of the Kulin Nation, and large carved ancestor stones.

Here there's a stop for kids, too, as you arrive at **ArtPlay** (melbourne.vic.gov.au/arts-and-culture/artplay/Pages/ArtPlay.aspx) with its cool playground along with workshops and performances within its historic red-brick railway building – a remnant from when this site was used as railway lines from 1856 before being redeveloped in 2002.

◉ **OTHERWISE MAKE YOUR WAY** past Birrarung Marr's open event space to pass under a pedestrian bridge where you'll veer off to the right up along the sloped path. Just up from here are the **Federation Bells** (federationbells.com.au): an intriguing orchestral art installation comprising 39 upturned bronze bells resembling something from another planet. They play a range of clamouring compositions throughout the day, which are either soothing or irritating depending on your mood (8am-9am, 12.30-1.30pm and 5-6pm). You can even compose a piece of your own, which you can sometimes upload online.

⊙ **NEXT** you'll cross over the **William Barak Bridge,** a shared pedestrian–cyclist path that spans a sprawling network of train lines connecting Melbourne's CBD with the 'burbs. But this ain't your ordinary bridge and it doubles as a sound art installation that gives voice to 53 artists from the Commonwealth nations, created as part of the 2006 games held here in Melbourne with both the **Melbourne Cricket Ground** (mcg.org.au) and **Melbourne and Olympic parks** (mopt.com.au) – the two areas that stand before you now – taking centre stage. And though it probably feels pretty relaxed at the moment, come footy season this spot is transformed into a sea of team colours as AFL fans stream over on the way to the ground. The bridge itself was named after William Barak (c. 1824–1903) an inspiring Wurundjeri-willam Elder, clan leader and artist who dedicated his life to campaigning for First Nations' rights while liaising between officials and his people.

⊙ **THE END OF THE BRIDGE** brings you to another inspiring figure, Neale Daniher, where a walk is named in honour of this former AFL footballer and coach whose efforts to raise funds for motor neurone disease take place here on the Queen's Birthday Melbourne v Collingwood clash. And though you're heading right for the 'G, before you reach the ground you'll take a sneaky right at the cricket nets (where both international and state teams warm up before games) to take the pedestrian bridge that heads over the train tracks as you follow the signs to **Rod Laver Arena** (rodlaverarena.com.au) down the steep path. Home to the Australian Open since 1988 (and countless rock concerts in between), it's named after Australian tennis legend Rod Laver, winner of 11 grand slam events and the only player to have twice won the Grand Slam (all four majors in the one year). Along with Laver's statue is the Australian Tennis Hall of Fame that's showcased in a row of bronze busts. Cycle through the complex of courts and stadiums to reach **John Cain Arena** (named after the 41st Victorian premier), which hosts Melbourne's National Basketball League and Super Netball matches.

⊖ **TIME TO PAUSE**, take a deep breath and flex the muscles as you need to lug your bike up a flight of stairs to cross over another footbridge back over the tracks before you land beneath the shadows of the mighty MCG. Known as the 'people's ground', this heritage-listed cricket and football ground opened in 1853 and remains Australia's largest stadium with a capacity of 100,000 people. (Fun fact: though it's had many a bumper crowd over the years, the record attendance was not for a sporting event but for US evangelist Billy Graham who crammed in 143,000 people back here in 1959.)

⊖ **ARRIVING** at the Shane Warne Stand (formerly the Great Southern Stand), cycle in an anti-clockwise direction around the hallowed turf as you pass a who's who of AFL and cricket legends – Bradman, Warne, Miller, Barassi, Matthews – among other sporting stars immortalised in bronze as part of the Parade of Champions. But it's at the Olympic Stand where you'll find golden girls Shirley Strickland and Betty Cuthbert, two of our finest track athletes, who won gold at the 1956 Melbourne Olympics that were held at this very ground. You can enter the ground itself, either do an **MCG Tour** for a behind-the-scenes look or visit the **Australian Sports Museum** (`australiansportsmuseum.org.au`) for interactive hands-on displays and plenty of priceless sporting memorabilia covering pretty much every sport ever played in Australia.

⊖ **INSIDE** there's some good coverage of First Nations sporting history too, from Cathy Freeman to Marngrook, a game played involving kicking around a possum skin ball that was the precursor to Australian Rules football. And this ties in nicely with your next stop as you leave the 'G to cycle through the expansive Yarra Park, following the sign towards Punt Road Oval, to reach a beautiful **scarred tree.**

Anywhere from 300 to 800 years old, this old river red gum offers a rare insight to pre-colonised Melbourne. Sitting behind a protective fence, the tree is an example of how the Wurundjeri People removed bark to make anything from canoes and shields to baby carriers.

⊙ **FROM HERE** cut through to link up with Sheffield Walk to exit the park at Punt Rd where you'll cross over at the lights to leave Melbourne's sporting precinct behind. Here the route enters a new phase as you're led through Richmond's once working-class backstreets turned multimillion-dollar rows. Head down **Rowena Pde** with its fine collection of Victorian terraces, Edwardian houses and workers' cottages as you keep an eye out for the heritage-listed old **Pelaco** shirts sign looming in the background, one of Richmond's iconic landmarks, a hark back to its manufacturing days when it produced iconic Aussie brands from Redheads matches to Rosella tomato sauce. Up ahead is **Rowena Parade Corner Store** (rowenacornerstore.com), an old milk bar in business since 1956. Though you'll no longer able to get a dollar's worth of mixed lollies and a bag of Whizz Fizz, you can get well-made coffees and contemporary Greek dishes at this much-loved cafe. Head around the side of the building to check out the outdoor mural tribute to Richmond premiership hero, Dustin Martin.

⊙ **CONTINUE ALONG** Rowena Pde until you reach the **Vaucluse**, a hoity-toity street so exclusive and leafy it's heritage-listed for being the last Victorian-era private street in inner Melbourne. Among its historic mansions you'll find some spectacular architecture, including St Kevin's ornate Waterford campus, the imposing bluestone St Ignatius Church and a red-brick parish, as well as the Melbourne Indigenous Transition School set up to assist students from remote communities.

⊙ **BACKTRACK TO Lennox St** and turn left at the roundabout past Lindberg Galleries (lindbergcontemporary.com.au) and a ghost sign to Hersh's Tailor, a 100-year-old business that operated up until the 1990s, before hitting one of Richmond's famed backstreet pubs, the **London Tavern** (londontavernhotel.com). Dating to 1921, this handsome red-brick boozer is one of Melbourne's great footy pubs. It brings in a rowdy crowd for pre- or post-game drinks, or to watch games live on TV, but at other times it's a relaxed spot to settle in at the front bar or beer garden for a counter meal and a cold beer. There's also has a handy hole-in-the-wall counter by Clarke St Coffee for an artisanal coffee to go.

⊙ **CONTINUE SOUTH** along Lennox St to reach **Swan St**, the heart and soul of old-school Richmond. And while gentrification has threatened to take away its inner-city character, today it's rediscovered its mojo with just enough grit to counterbalance the yuppified touches. Here's about the halfway mark, so lock up the bike and go for a stroll to admire its heritage-lined facade of old shopfronts, including the iconic Dimmey's department store clock tower –if you're after cheap jocks and socks you'll be disappointed instead to find it's now luxury apartments. But as consolation there are stops for gelato (`gelatomessina.com/stores/richmond` or `piccolinagelateria.com.au`), gourmet deli sandwiches (`hugosdeli.com.au`), books (`avenuebookstore.com.au`) and wine (`attria.com.au`). And of course there are plenty of pubs too, including the **Corner Hotel** (`cornerhotel.com`), one of Melbourne's finest rock'n'roll venues, where anyone and everyone from the White Stripes to Mick Jagger has graced its stage. While it's likely way too early for a gig, you can settle in at its divey front bar, its boisterous rooftop bar, or, in the warmer months, its Round the Corner taqueria with sports on the big screen.

⊙ **BACK ON THE BIKE AGAIN**, make your way north-west along Stewart St, along the back of Richmond station, where you should 'do yourself a favour' and check out the statue of music guru (and local Richmond identity) **Molly Meldrum**. Here he's posing with his trademark hat and his beloved pooch, Ziggy, whose inclusion was a deal-maker in the statue going ahead. Admire the murals as you zip past the atmospheric old red-brick textiles factories, including Australian Knitting Mills (AKM), that, like most of Richmond, developers have converted to hip warehouse apartments and studios. At the end of the street you'll pass **Total Rush** (`totalrush.cc`) who can help out with bike repairs, accessories and caffeine from their bike shop/cafe.

⊚ **BACK AT PUNT RD** – thankful not to be caught in its notorious peak-hour gridlock – cross over at the lights to land yourself on Brunton Ave, where you'll make your way past the Richmond footy club's training base. Skirting Yarra Park, you'll next reach the 19th-century **Cabman's Shelter**, an interesting snippet of history where horse-cart drivers would snooze after knock-off drinks. This one was originally placed near Parliament House before being moved here in more recent years.

⊚ **HERE** take the footbridge to nip back over the railway to return to Melbourne's sporting precinct at Olympic Blvd. You'll land at the distinctive bubble-dome stadium of **AAMI Park** (aamipark.com.au) – home to Melbourne's soccer and rugby teams. Just to your right is **Olympic Park**, an athletics track with a fascinating history. Starting out as the site of Melbourne's first zoo in 1861, it was later developed into 'Melbourne Motordrome', a race circuit so dangerous it was known as Suicide Track. Even more insane was its attempt to host ostrich races – an event the papers unsurprisingly described as being 'a complete fiasco'. It was then developed into a velodrome where the legendary cyclist Sir Hubert Opperman covered 100 miles (161 km) in 90 minutes. But arguably it's most famous for where John Landy stopped to help fallen runner Ron Clarke in 1956, in doing so sacrificing his chance of breaking the world record – but all the while somehow still managing to win the race! It's a moment you'll find immortalised here in bronze, an enduring symbol of good sportsmanship that the Sport Australia Hall of Fame named as the nation's finest sporting moment of the 20th century.

⊚ **FROM HERE** make your way down alongside Gosch's Paddock, once the domain of cows and horses and now the AFL training facility for Melbourne Football Club. Soon you'll meet the Morrell Pedestrian Bridge, leading over the M1 freeway, where you'll spot the iconic (and non-functioning) Nylex Clock, a much-loved part of Melbourne's skyline that sits atop old grain silos. And though it's been on the blink since 2009, when Nylex (a plastics manufacturer who created another Aussie icon, the Esky) went into liquidation, this heritage-listed clock briefly told

Melburnians the time and temperature again when vandals broke in 2015 to flick the switch back on!

⊙ **ONCE YOU HIT THE RIVER,** take a right to join the north bank of the Yarra Trail back into the city as the city's rowers glide by. To your right across Batman Ave is the AIA Centre, a swimming venue used in the 1956 Olympics (the last original remaining building from the games) before becoming the Glass House basketball stadium and today part of the training complex for Collingwood Football Club – the team everyone loves to hate.

⊙ **THE TRAIL GOES BENEATH** Swan St Bridge as it passes the tennis centre to take you to the final stretch. Just before you return to Birrarung Marr, keep an eye out for **Speaker's Corner.** About 50m off the path is this complex of stone mounds that date backs to the 1880s, where, before Facebook and Twitter, crowds would gather to cheer and jeer those here to express their views on anything from communism, religion and anti-conscription to women's suffrage. (Note: while folk no longer people come here to vent their views, if you're interested, 'Speakers' Forum' still goes on outside the State Library of Victoria on Sundays at 3pm).

⚑ **AS YOU REACH** Birrarung Marr's lowest terrace, stop at the iconic two-headed **Angel** sculpture to take a sweaty selfie framed by the city's attractive backdrop. It's then along past the river gums and Moreton Bay figs to arrive back at Federation Square, from where your options for onward exploration are endless.

CLICK, READ, LISTEN AND WATCH:

- 🌐 home.vicnet.net.au/~rbhs
- 📖 Janet McCalman, *Struggletown: Public and Private Life in Richmond 1900–1965*
- 🎵 Paul Kelly and the Coloured Girls, 'Leaps and Bounds'
  Greg Champion, 'That's the Thing about Football'

PORT MELBOURNE, SOUTH MELBOURNE & ALBERT PARK

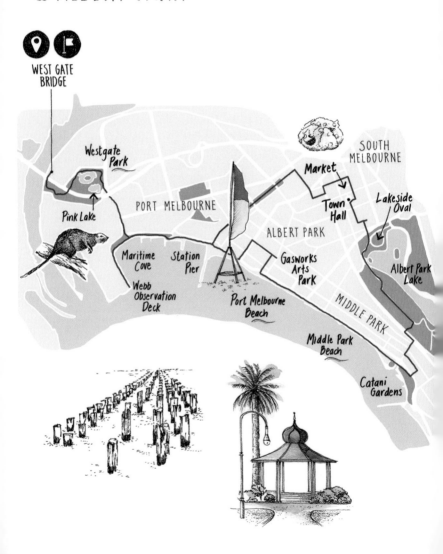

WEST GATE
BRIDGE

Westgate
Park

Pink Lake

PORT MELBOURNE

Market

SOUTH
MELBOURNE

Town
Hall

Lakeside
Oval

ALBERT PARK

Maritime
Cove

Station
Pier

Gasworks
Arts
Park

Albert Park
Lake

Webb
Observation
Deck

Port Melbourne
Beach

MIDDLE PARK

Middle Park
Beach

Catani
Gardens

START // FINISH	DISTANCE
West Gate Bridge	Approximately 22km one-way

DURATION
half- to full-day

TRANSPORT
To reach the West Gate Bridge, take the train to Spotswood from where you can take the punt across the Yarra to begin the ride

CONNECTING RIDES
Bay Trail (p40)
Capital City Trail (p28)
Hobsons Bay Coastal Trail (p52)
Sandridge Trail

Offering a lovely balance between bike path and backstreet ramble is this jam-packed day pedalling through Melbourne's inner southern suburbs. It's a ride that offers a different slant on the city as you're led down a route mixing fascinating history with pretty bayside beaches, grand 19th-century architecture, some superb parkland and plenty of breaks for food, swims and local culture.

While hanging out beneath the **West Gate Bridge** may not sound like your idea of fun, hear us out on this one. Not only is this the gateway to two of Melbourne's great rides, the **Hobsons Bay Coastal Trail** (p52) and the **Bay Trail** (p40), but it may surprise you to learn there's a wetlands nature reserve down here too. Beyond that, it gives you the unique perspective of standing beneath the towering pylons of this Melbourne landmark – and getting here is an interesting ride in itself. It's a route that takes you through Port Melbourne's Fishermans Bend (via the Yarra River Esplanade before joining Lorimer St) an area famous for manufacturing anything from Holden cars (sadly, no more) and Vegemite to World War II bombers, the latter in a building in which Boeing now produces its 787 Dreamliner aeroplanes.

CYCLING WITH KIDS: Enjoy a swim between stops for building sandcastles and tucking into fish and chips or ice-cream on any of the beaches. On Sundays, kids can take a **pony ride** at St Kilda West's Catani Gardens. Inland, take a spin on the Grand Prix track at **Albert Park** before snacking on a dim sim at the **South Melbourne Market.** Then it's either back to Port Melbourne or onward to Flinders St.

AND FROM THE BRIDGE you'll set off along the industrial banks of the Yarra to reach **Westgate Park** (`parks.vic.gov.au/places-to-see/parks/westgate-park`). Managed by Parks Victoria, with the assistance of not-for-profit **Westgate Biodiverity** (`westgatebiodiversity.org.au`), a great job has been done here in regenerating this wasteland into natural wetlands comprising native grasses and coastal saltmarsh to lure back native birdlife. But it's the salt **pink lake** that it's most known for. And given the industrial area, you could be forgiven for thinking this psychedelic pink water is because of a toxic spill, but instead it's an all-natural phenomenon that occurs during hot spells of weather when algae grows in its salt crust to produce the garish pink pigment. Though far from a regular event (in fact it's more likely than not to be an underwhelming brown), when it is glowing it's quite the attraction with the selfie-snapping set. Here the lake is framed by the 2583m-long bridge, and as you look out over the endless stream of cars (there are an extraordinary 205,000-plus vehicles each day!) give thought to the tragic day when 35 workers lost their lives when, during its construction, the West Gate collapsed in 1970; the event remains the nation's worst industrial accident.

 FROM THE LAKE you'll exit the park to follow the dedicated bike path under the foot of the West Gate. Head down gritty Todd Rd, where among factories and endless freight trucks the bay looms ahead like a mirage.

 ARRIVING AT Maritime Cove, the beach here would be quite attractive if it weren't for the jarring backdrop of a container terminal with cranes busy loading up at Webb Docks. So let's just say it has character, but perhaps it's best to pass on having a swim here. The cafe at the surf lifesaving club is a bonus if you're wanting a coffee before taking a right for a detour along a boardwalk trail that curves around the bay. Here there's a maritime-themed playground – if kids are in tow – before you reach **Webb Observation Deck** for unique views over the city skyline and Port Phillip Bay/Nerm.

RETRACE YOUR ROUTE to join up with the Bay Trail, stopping to read about **rakali**, a native rodent that lives in burrows along the shoreline here. These furry critters, which have webbed hind legs and waterproof fur, have undergone a public image makeover in recent years to be rebadged with the Ngarrindjeri name, replacing the less appealing 'water rat' they were previously called.

CRUISE ALONG Port Melbourne's foreshore reserve where high-rise apartments spring up like it's Surfers Paradise, before arriving at the historic **Princes Pier**. Completed in 1915, it was here where the Anzacs bid farewell to loved ones before embarking on their long, perilous journey to battlefields of World Wars I and II; and where the fortunate ones were greeted upon return. Cycle out along the 580m-long pier to pass the quaint gatehouse (c. 1935) and its endpoint where anglers cast a line among the 'forest of piles', hundreds of remnant pier piles rising from the water like an abstract art piece.

Princes Pier was also a major gateway for postwar immigrants, but it's the next pier along where most of Melbourne's arrivals first laid eyes on their new homeland. Opening in 1854, **Station Pier** is where anyone from English and European  immigrants to those chancing their luck during the gold rush took their first steps on Australian land. But it was the years between 1949 and 1966 that saw a huge surge in numbers, when an average of 61,000 immigrants arrived each year after World War II – from displaced persons across war-torn Europe to those lured here as part of the government's immigration scheme. The latter group including many immigrants from Italy and Greece, which explains their integral part of Melbourne's multicultural make-up. From here they'd jump straight on the train along the old Sandridge Line that ran to Flinders Street station (from where many would continue to Bonegilla). And though that train line was decommissioned in 1987, the heritage-listed station remains as part of what is now the 109 light rail that runs to Box Hill via the city. It's also the starting point for the **Sandridge Rail Trail**, allowing cyclists to link up with the city.

If you're wondering what the lighthouse-like beacon sitting 100m out in the bay is, it's one of the two heritage-listed **Port Melbourne Lead Lights**: original 1924 channel markers for ships heading along this route into Port Melbourne. And where's the second one, you may ask? Turn around and you'll see it right behind you, about 450m inland in a park. It may seem like a strange place for it but this is its original location to assist guiding ships passing through the night.

⊜ **AT THIS POINT** you may be getting peckish, in which case you'll find a contender for Melbourne's best fish and chips at **D'lish Fish** (dlishfish.com), along with several restaurants set inside the pier, but otherwise rest assured there are plenty of scenic eating options ahead.

And for those who love to bag out Melbourne's beaches (we're looking at you, Sydneysiders), clearly you haven't dropped by on a balmy summer's evening to see its sparkling string of inner-city beaches stretching from Port Melbourne, South Park and Middle Beach to famed **St Kilda Beach** (p44); with that said, do check the Environment Protection Agency's website for a water report before swimming . . .

This coastline is where the Yalukit-willam, a clan of the Boonwurrung People, have resided for many thousands of years. This was a time when, before high-rise apartments, it was covered in tea tree and encroached on by wetlands that were a rich hunting ground where the local people could find kangaroos, fish, eels and myrrnong (tubers). Keep an eye out for stops along the cultural map to read about local First Nations landmarks, histories and traditions.

⊙ **BUT BEFORE YOU REACH** the main beaches, you can't visit Port Melbourne without a quick look down **Bay St**. So duck across the road to ride pass the Art Deco Pier Port for a change of scene as you find yourself among this strip of heritage pubs, cafes and gelatarias; bear in mind the best half of Bay St is a bit up from here. Cycle a couple of blocks to take a right into Graham St past a row of cute workers' cottages that serve as reminder of the days when this used to be a working-class suburb of dockers and wharfies. Ride by the **Graham Hotel** (thegrahamhotel.com.au), a handsome backstreet boozer that's been here for over 150 years and current-day gastropub believed to be haunted by the ghost of a sex worker murdered upstairs. You'll soon arrive at **Gasworks Arts Park** (gasworks.org.au), the former South Melbourne Gas Plant that opened in 1873 and ran till 1957, powered by coal that came in via horse-drawn trams from the old Station Pier. Today it's an art precinct comprising galleries, studios and a theatre, set on 3ha of parkland. If you're around on a Saturday, there's a farmers' market too (8am to 1pm).

⊙ **BACKTRACK** to turn left into quiet Johnston St to link back up with the Bay Trail at **Port Melbourne Life Saving Club** (portmelblsc.com.au). **Port Melbourne's beach** stretches along the palm-lined boulevard across from an eclectic mix of heritage and modern apartments that look out over the bay. Next along is **South Melbourne Beach** where its century-old lifesaving club has received a slick architectural makeover and looks out to manicured sands popular with swimmers, sunbathers and those here for the beach volleyball courts who bring an energetic SoCal atmosphere, albeit without the surf.

● **IF AT THIS POINT** the kids are getting a bit over it, the **Plum Garland Memorial Playground** appears as a much-needed distraction with its beachfront swings, slides and climbing frames. Failing that, ice-cream will do the trick, and fortunately **Jock's Ice Cream & Sorbet** (facebook.com/pages/Jocks-Ice-Cream-And-Sorbet/154426657924403) is just a short ride away for anything from Obamarama (peanut butter with berry ripple) to Pavlova among other seasonal and classic flavours. To get here, head north along Victoria Ave through this villagey strip of Albert Park, where if you're keen to venture further, you'll come across other local institutions such as **Andrew's Hamburgers** (andrewshamburgers.com.au), which has been sizzling up its old-school burgers since 1939 – they're every bit as good as the hype – and **Misuzus** for classy contemporary Japanese.

But fair enough if you have an appetite for something more 'beachy' and Middle Park's aptly named **Sandbar** (sandbarbeachcafe.com.au) delivers with its prime beachfront location where you can tuck into anything from calamari salad to all-day breakfasts, while enjoying the sand in between your toes.

And if you're wondering whose pair of boots and clothes that is draped over the bluestone seawall nearby, well, they belong to some bloke called Tommy, and here is his story – one that's immortalised in bronze. A sculpture by Bill Perrin, *Tommy's Story* is dedicated to a local wharfie who, back in the days of the Great Depression, would choose to swim to work, not just to save money by not taking public transport, but also not to have to take a bath – heating water was expensive in those days!

● **FURTHER ALONG** is our vote for the bay's best beach at **Middle Park**, for its laid-back feel and long uninterrupted stretch, before reaching **St Kilda West Beach** with its waterfront bistro, **West Beach Pavilion** (westbeachstkilda.com.au), an old beach bathing pavilion dating from the 1920s. During summer it's transformed into a happening beach bar, complete with cabanas and sunbeds, but if that all sounds a bit trendy, just grab a table on the sand for pizzas and house-made jugs of sangria.

⊘ **FROM HERE** the Bay Trail veers off down to the foreshore, at which point you'll keep going straight to pass by the heritage-listed **Catani Gardens.** This attractive landscaped park is filled with stately palms and historical monuments, and on Sundays there are pony rides for the kids. It was all part of the master plan to beautify St Kilda's foreshore, a job first given to Italian-born Carlo Catani back in the early 1900s.

⊘ **IT'S A FITTING PLACE** to mark the halfway point. Here you'll leave the bike trail to embark on your return via the inner-city backstreets as you cross over Beaconsfield Pde to pedal through St Kilda West's glorious, leafy residential streets. Prepare for 'house envy' levels to skyrocket; these elegant heritage houses are all within a Frisbee fling from the beach. Make your way along Mary St to turn left into Park St, before turning right at the roundabout at Cowderoy St to pass the family-friendly **Cowderoy's Dairy** (`cowderoysdairy.com.au`) a former milk bar dating to 1932 turned well-loved neighbourhood cafe inside a beautiful Art Deco building. Continue on through the next roundabout to turn left into Canterbury Rd as you keep your eyes peeled for the **Pamela Anderson house**, a local landmark fronted by a blue mural of the *Baywatch* bombshell, a piece controversially commissioned by then owner, and former footballer/media personality, Sam Newman.

⊘ **CROSS OVER** at the Fraser St light rail station to weave your way through the footy ovals to land on Aughtie Dr, where it's 'pedal to metal' as you find yourself on the pit straight of Albert Park's Formula One track. This is where the **Australian Grand Prix** has been held since Jeff Kennett poached it from Adelaide in 1996, and along with Monaco and a handful of others, it's one of the few street circuits on the F1 calendar where a public road is used a racetrack. Ahead you'll ride by the team pits (the only permanent structure along the track) where you'll envisage yourself passing the chequered flag where the likes of Schumacher and Hamilton have done so many times before. And though the race returned in the mid-90s, the first race held here was back in the 1950s when the likes of Jack Brabham and Stirling Moss raced around this lake circuit. A few bends ahead is when **Albert Park Lake** itself comes into view, one of Melbourne's most scenic attractions, with its sparkling waters popular with rowers and sailors as much as they are with swans and ducks. The waters were once a tributary linked to the Yarra, and it's believed these former wetlands were as diverse as Kakadu National Park; the Yalukit-willam People would camp nearby in bark shelters 30,000 years prior to any F1 car screaming around here.

◉ **ON YOUR WAY OUT** the Albert Park Lake complex, you'll ride by the old **Lakeside Oval**, the ground where South Melbourne Swans played games from 1897 till relocating to Sydney in 1982 (and also where the 1901 grand final was played).

◉ **CROSS OVER** Albert Road to find yourself back in South Melbourne, riding along **Clarendon St**, which is lined with restaurants, cafes and pubs. Ride north a couple of blocks before turning right into Raglan St to take a look at **The See Yup temple** (76 Raglan St) an ornate Chinese temple that dates to 1856, and housed within a Classical Revival-style building.

◉ **BACK ON** Clarendon, make your way along the other side of Raglan St to ride by its Victorian terrace houses, before taking a right at Church St where at the corner of Napier St is the **Temperance Hall** (temperancehall.com.au). Built in 1863 by the Abstinence Society (who'd be aghast to find how many pubs there are now in South Melbourne), it's now a theatre for LGBTQIA+ experimental dance and performance. Glide on through Church St to arrive at Park St's wonderful 19th-century streetscape that marks an area known as **Emerald Hill**. Check out the grand old Patross Knitting Mills building with its turreted tower before weaving along through Perrins St to continue to the palatial **South Melbourne Town Hall** (c. 1879).

Continue around to return back to Clarendon St as you pass countless restaurants and some artisanal boutiques, while saving up your appetite for **South Melbourne Market** (southmelbournemarket.com.au). Established in 1867, the market closes kinda early (around 4pm) and is also closed Mondays, Tuesday and Thursday, so hopefully you've timed your run to sample the one thing all first-timers are here for: the South Melbourne Market Dim Sim. Who would've thought that a recipe by a Mr William Wing Young back in the 1940s would turn out to become a Melbourne icon! And though you can find the humble 'dimmie' all over now, the best is still here: the original South Melbourne version. Failing that, **Claypots Evening Star** (`facebook.com/claypotseveningstar`) is open daily for you to enjoy Mediterranean-inspired seafood at its atmospheric bar.

◉ **RIDING ON,** no doubt now burping up dimmies, you'll lug your bike down the stairs over the historic South Melbourne light rail station to ride along Coventry St to reach a **Portable Iron House** (`nationaltrust.org.au/places/portable-iron-houses`) – a gold rush-era dwelling that's one of the few remaining prefabricated iron houses in the world; there were once hundreds found around these streets.

⚑ **TURN RIGHT** into Montague St for a 500m dash along what's quite a busy road (so take care) to reach its notorious namesake low bridge that snares many an unsuspecting truck each year. But unless you're a giant riding a penny-farthing, you shouldn't have much to worry about. And here's where you'll join up with the Sandridge Rail Trail to glide along this designated bike path that follows the old train line (and current light rail) for around 2km all the way back to Station Pier – from where it's about 4km to return to where it all started under the West Gate Bridge. Alternatively, you can take the rail trail the other way to head into Southbank in the city, where you'll work your way to the Travellers Bridge, an appropriate way to complete the ride in honour of the many immigrants who've helped build Melbourne into the marvellous city it is today.

CLICK, READ, LISTEN AND WATCH:

🌐 Port Melbourne Historical & Preservation Society
(pmhps.org.au)

📖 James Morton and Russell Robinson, *Shotgun and Standover: The story of the Painters and Dockers*

🎵 Icecream Hands, 'Gasworks Park'
Mark Seymour, 'Westgate'

PRAHRAN, ST KILDA & WINDSOR

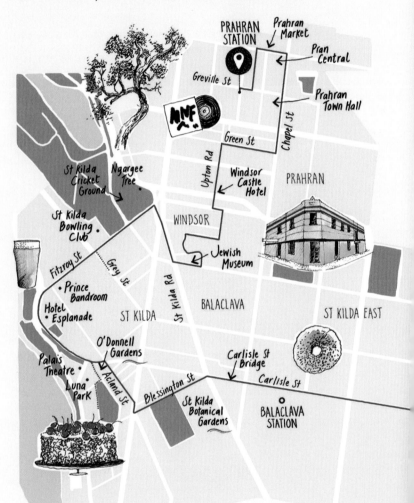

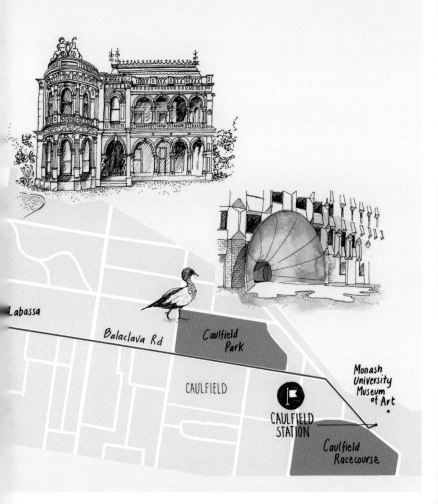

Labassa

Balaclava Rd

Caulfield Park

CAULFIELD

CAULFIELD STATION

Monash University Museum of Art

Caulfield Racecourse

START		**DISTANCE**	
Prahran station		14.5km one-way	
FINISH		**DURATION**	
Caulfield station		Half- to full-day	

CONNECTING RIDES

Bay Trail (p40)

TRANSPORT
Start off at Prahran,
Balaclava or Windsor stations

This joyous ride leads you through the storied backstreets of St Kilda with First Nations heritage, Eastern European flavour and all of the suburb's infamous grit and glamour, as well as passing through the more chic streets of Prahran and Windsor. Take this journey through the ups and downs of one of Melbourne's most famous suburbs, where historic grandeur and seaside festivities sit alongside bohemian flair and a seedy past.

WHILE 'SEX, DRUGS AND ROCK'N'ROLL' is not usually used to describe something as wholesome as a bike ride, for one through St Kilda it's fitting. Though these days it's much tamer, affluent and, some original locals would argue, less exciting than the debauched drug-fuelled days when Nick Cave and co. were 'kicking against the pricks', here you'll find a cultural legacy that still burns bright through these fabled streets.

CYCLING WITH KIDS: At the **Prahran Market**, kids will drool over cupcakes and enjoy regular kid-friendly events (prahranmarket.com.au/whats-on). In St Kilda, visit the **Jewish Museum** and a First Nations **scarred tree**. Allow plenty of time for **Luna Park. Acland Street** beckons with cake shops and gelato; **Readings** has plenty of quality kids' books. Possibly even find time for a movie (barefootcinema.com.au/st-kilda), or ride back along the bay trail to **St Kilda Pier** to look for the little penguins at dusk.

● **YOU'LL KICK THINGS OFF** in Prahran, an inner-city suburb celebrated for its diversity and nightlife – and Greville St makes for a stylish first impression. These days it's less grunge and more chic, but **Greville Records** (grevillerecords.com.au) is still one of Melbourne's best independent music stores; after more than 40 years in operation, it remains the last bastion from the punk era.

● **FROM HERE** take a sneaky left into Izett St for the short ride to **Prahran Market** (prahranmarket.com.au). Dating back to 1864, this much-loved foodie destination is as popular today for its coffee (marketlane.com.au), delis and street food as it is for fresh produce. Stock up on all manner of gourmet goods and make your way east along busy Commercial Rd, taking care to avoid trams and errant car doors, to pass by the monumental seven-storey Edwardian baroque department store that's now **Pran Central** (prancentral.com.au).

● **THEN TAKE A RIGHT** onto one of Melbourne's most famous streets, the oh-so grand and glittery (yet kinda gritty) **Chapel St**, a resplendent strip of heritage buildings that, depending on what time you visit, will offer different vibes. By day, this Prahran and Windsor end is all about food and shopping, especially vintage clothing. You can stop by the wonderful **Chapel St Bazaar** (facebook.com/ChapelStreetBazaar) for all your paisley and bell-bottom needs. Come night, it's abuzz with a hedonistic crowd here for clubbing, bars and restaurants, all to the soundtrack of doof-doof blaring from car subwoofers doing 'mainsies'.

● **RIDE BY** the majestic **Prahran Town Hall** (1861) admiring its ornate clock tower before crossing over High St into the more hip suburb of **Windsor**. Keep an eye out for **Betty's Burgers** (bettysburgers.com.au), the one lone building in all of Melbourne to receive substantial damage from Victoria's major earthquake in 2021 (but all publicity is good publicity, right?), where you'll take a right into Green St to leave Chapel St behind. Cut through the back streets to find a mix of Victorian terraces, Edwardian and Art Deco houses, and what becomes a more relaxed ride. If you've ever fantasised about running away to join the circus, here's where you can make it happen as you pass by **NICA** (National Institute of Circus Arts; nica.com.au), Australia's only university for circus performers.

⮕ **TAKE A LEFT** into Upton Rd to pass **Upton Girl** (instagram.com/uptongirl_) one of Melbourne's old milk bars converted into a cafe, before riding through a succession of roundabouts to reach the **Windsor Castle Hotel** (windsorcastle.com.au). If you thought the lime-green colour scheme was the most distinctive thing about this old local favourite pub, take a look up to see the pink elephants on the roof. Relax: no one's spiked your drink; they've been up here for decades, so well-known in fact that one was stolen (which is no easy feat), only to turn up seven years later chained to a pole down the road!

⮕ **FROM HERE** Upton Rd flies over six lanes of traffic to land you in **St Kilda.** These leafy streets make for a genteel introduction for a suburb with a so-called seedy reputation, as you take a left into Wellington St, a right at Crimea St and right again into mansion-lined Charnwood Rd. At Charnwood Grove take a right to curve around the heritage-listed **St Kilda Hebrew Congregation Synagogue** (stkildashule.org.au), a striking architectural piece dating from the 1920s and built in a Byzantine Revival style. Take a left at Charnwood Cres to swing around Alma Rd and arrive at the **Jewish Museum** (jewishmuseum.com.au). Here you'll learn of another fascinating chapter in multicultural Melbourne's history: of the many Jewish immigrants who settled here from the mid-19th century to post–World War II – including some 8000 Holocaust survivors (one of the largest groups outside Israel) – to make up an integral part of St Kilda's social fabric.

⮕ **NEXT** you'll run the gauntlet along busy St Kilda Rd (stick to the bike lane and you'll be fine) for a short ride to St Kilda Junction to reach another important cultural sight, the beautiful **Ngargee Tree.** Hidden away in a small bush-filled corner of the Junction Oval, this 20m-tall red gum is a sacred meeting place for the Yalukit-willam and Boonwurrung Peoples, the Traditional Owners who've lived here for millennia. Estimated to be 300 to 500 years old, this is the last tree of a forest that spanned into Prahran and where First Nations people gathered for cultural ceremonies well before European settlement in 1835.

This is part of the south-east corner of Albert Park, including the **St Kilda Cricket Ground**, a heritage-listed ground established 1856. Used as a secondary ground by the Victorian state team (and for the occasional Big Bash T20 game) it's here where the late, great Shane Warne (1969-2022) first cut his teeth as a young leggie playing grade cricket for St Kilda. It was also used for footy, most notably as the Saints' home ground until they relocated to the 'animal enclosure' in Moorabbin in 1964.

⊘ **YOU'RE NOW IN** the heart of St Kilda, **Fitzroy St**, famous as much for its historical grandeur as it is for its sordid past. A dedicated bike path runs along its length of endless landmarks. First up is the heritage-listed **St Kilda Bowling Club** (established 1865) which was featured regularly on the TV show *The Secret Life of Us* and was the first place to 'get the ball rolling' in luring in a younger, hipper crowd for what we know now as barefoot bowls.

⊘ **NEXT ALONG** is **St Kilda station** and, though it hasn't seen a train since 1987, it remains Victoria's oldest railway station dating to 1857. These days it's an Irish pub (thefifthprovince.com.au) as well as a tram stop for the 96 into the city.

⊘ **SITTING PRETTY** across Fitzroy St is the regal **George Hotel**, a historic four-level Italianate 19th-century landmark. Going by its grandiose appearance, you'd never guess this was home to Melbourne's famed punk scene in the late '70s. Known as the Crystal Ballroom, back then it was the epicentre for local and Australian underground bands to play, where anyone from Nick Cave's Boys Next Door and the Birthday Party to the Saints, Go Betweens and INXS would tear it apart, along with internationals such as Iggy Pop, The Gun Club and The Cure. But well before the punks were in pogo-ing and gobbing on stage, the George was a posh resort and ballroom, attracting only the most respectable members of society. Today it's been returned to its original splendour as a ballroom wedding venue, while the old snake pit has also been refurbed as the **George Lounge** (thegeorgelounge.com.au), and George Lane (georgelane.com.au) is around the back for live gigs. Just up from here you can pay your respects at **Roland S Howard Lane** (located just off Grey St down Eildon St) named after the much-respected Melbourne guitarist who played in the Birthday Party, Boys Next Door and These Immortal Souls.

St Kilda's after-dark reputation also extends to the red light district of **Grey St**, an area associated with sex workers ever since American soldiers were stationed here during World War II. While the ladies of the night still frequent the area, these days it's more drunken backpackers who are the main scourge to local residents. But above all it's a street known for stately architecture and mansions. Just off Grey St is **Wattle House** (53 Jackson St), St Kilda's oldest surviving house, built in 1847 and a rare example of pre-gold-rush architecture.

➲ **RETURN TO** Fitzroy St's bike path to continue your tour of this fascinating street as you pass the **Tolarno Hotel** (tolarnostkilda.com.au). This is a bona fide St Kilda classic that was a bohemian hangout from the 1960s and has since been heritage listed as a cultural site. It was made famous by 'it' couple artist Mirka Mora and her restaurateur/galley owner husband, Georges Mora, who opened up their home as a restaurant, studio and gallery to attract a cast of all weird and wonderful locals. Today it's a hotel, but their legacy remains via artworks displayed throughout.

➲ **JUST A FEW DOORS ALONG** is – *was* – the Gatwick Hotel (thegatwickhotel.com). If ever there was a symbol for St Kilda's crass gentrification, this is it. This Art Deco landmark had long served as a halfway boarding house for down-at-heel locals suffering social issues and drug addiction until it was sold in 2019 for reality TV show *The Block* to flip as luxury apartments; many former residents now sleep rough on the streets.

⊙ **ACROSS FROM** the Gatwick is one of Fitzroy Street's few contemporary buildings, the striking **Victoria Pride Centre** (`pridecentre.org.au`) built specifically for the LGBTQIA+ community. It's a symbol of St Kilda's long-standing role as a place for celebrating diversity, and you can drop by to check out its downstairs gallery and cafe.

⊙ **ALONG A BIT FROM HERE** is another local St Kilda rock'n'roll icon, the **Prince Bandroom** (`theprince.com.au/prince-bandroom`). Fortunately the venue formerly known as the Prince of Wales is still kicking; everyone from Henry Rollins and TISM to Coldplay and P!nk has played upstairs. As well as music, this beautiful Art Deco building (c. 1936) has also played an important part in embracing the local LGBTQIA+ community, and has an interesting place in history as the temporary headquarters of the United States military officers' club in World War II. And though Prince of Wales barflies will bemoan the loss of its divey front bar, at least we can be grateful it's still a place to get a beer and has not been converted to apartments.

⊙ **AT THIS POINT** Fitzroy St curves around to open out to St Kilda's famous sparkling foreshore. For many this right here is the real reason to come: the beach. Ahead you can join up with the **Bay Trail bike path** (p40) to check out all its beachfront landmarks, but in the meantime we're sticking to the upper embankment along the palm-lined Esplanade. Here you'll reach another vital piece of St Kilda's rock'n'roll story as you park alongside what is the most famous of them all: the **Hotel Esplanade** (`hotelesplanade.com.au`), simply known as the Espy. Set within a grand historic hotel overlooking the bay, where Mark Twain once stayed back in the 1880s, this legendary venue remains, despite its recent slick makeover, one of Melbourne's best for live music with a who's who of Aussie and international alternative/indie bands having played here. And you can't come this far without having a drink in the Espy, so pop in for a cold refreshment and a feed in its main bar, or from 4pm you can check out its upstairs cocktail bar named after resident ghost, Alfred Felton: a philanthropist and art collector who died up here in 1904.

🔿 **BACK IN THE SADDLE**, enjoy the sea breeze as you lap up the foreshore's festive atmosphere, where on Sundays you'll find the **St Kilda Esplanade Market** (`stkildaesplanademarket.com.au`). Contemplate how much it'd cost to live in one of those Art Deco apartments before you arrive at another jewel in St Kilda's crown, the superb **Palais Theatre** (`palaistheatre.com.au`). Built in the 1920s as picture theatre, it's hosted major acts from the Rolling Stones, Bob Dylan and the Strokes to performances by Opera Australia and the Kirov Ballet.

The Palais makes up part of the St Kilda Triangle (a long-term redevelopment project that's getting nowhere), alongside **Luna Park** (`lunapark.com.au`), Melbourne's very own version of Coney Island. This is the face of St Kilda: a big garish, smiling one (and frankly, kinda terrifying) in the form of Mr Moon, whose giant mouth fronts Luna Park's famous entrance gates. Opening in 1912, this kitschy theme park is most famous for its rickety old Scenic Railway, the oldest continually operated roller-coaster in the world.

🔿 **OUT FRONT** are the attractive palm-filled **O'Donnell Gardens** where you can take a breather on *Aunty Alma's Seat*, a series of bronze-cast milk crates dedicated to the First Nations peoples who've gathered here in a modern-day meeting place. Created by sculptor Julie Shiels, the piece came about after a chat with First Nations Elder Alma Roach (sister of musician Archie Roach) who, after mentioning how tough it was to find the milk crates they used for seating, inspired the idea for this 'anti monument' to be installed as a permanent fixture. Around the corner from here is **Peanut Farm Reserve**, a footy oval that's also a registered Yalukit-willam tool site, and features a mural of young local First Nations footballers created by renowned street artist Adnate (adnate.com.au). And if you're wondering about the name, it's because this area was once a peanut farm, back in World War II. Access it via Spenser St around the corner from the **Veg Out Community Gardens St Kilda** (vegout.org.au), which has a **farmers' market** (vegoutfarmersmarket.org.au) the first Saturday of each month.

⊙ **FROM HERE** you'll briefly return to St Kilda's back streets as you cross the tram tracks to head along Acland St while riding by the much-loved **Dogs Bar** (dogsbar.com.au), very much a local institution round this way. Then ride through the roundabout to reach **Linden New Art** (lindenarts.org), a gallery housed in an opulent double-storey Victorian mansion dating to 1871 and featuring contemporary art exhibitions.

⊙ **SWING BACK DOWN Acland St** to follow the tram tracks along this famous strip that's a showcase of local favourites – The **Vineyard** (thevineyard.com.au) for outdoor fun and frivolities; the **Memo Music Hall** (memomusichall.com.au) for live music; and the old-school **St Kilda RSL** (skanc.com.au) keeping it real. And if you like cakes, you've definitely come to the right place; Acland St is known for its Polish bakeries including **Monarch Cakes** (monarchcakes.com.au), who've been making their popular baked cheesecake and Chocolate Kooglhoupf here since 1934, and **Europa Cakes** (europacakeshop.com.au) who likewise have been at it for over 40 years. But if ice-cream is more your thing you're in luck too, with **Piccolina Gelateria** (piccolinagelateria.com.au) whipping up authentic Italian flavours to follow on from a meal of contemporary Italian at **Cicciolina** (cicciolina.com.au) across the road. Other stalwarts along here include **Readings** (readings.com.au), one of Melbourne's finest bookstores.

⊙ **FROM** Barkly St glide down Blessington to reach the heritage-listed **St Kilda Botanical Gardens**, which were established back in 1859. It's a good spot to escape the madding crowds, and among its well-tended gardens are chess tables and a Rain Man sculpture (not Dustin Hoffman's character, but a guy holding an umbrella in the middle of the pond). In February the **Barefoot Cinema** (`barefootcinema.com.au/st-kilda`) is held here if you want to come back early evening.

🡢 **EXIT** the gardens at the far end of Blessington St to continue along this leafy street to cross over the Nepean Hwy where St Kilda's Town Hall sits on Carlisle St's corner looking as lavish as the White House. Along Carlisle you'll ride by the **Local Taphouse** (`thelocal.com.au`) who were pouring craft beer well before it was even called 'craft beer' and then reconnect with Chapel St, albeit a low-key version.

🡢 **YOU'RE NOW IN** the suburb of **Balaclava**, an area most associated with Melbourne's Orthodox Jewish Community who you'll likely see getting about on foot. And if you're keen for some Jewish food, look no further then **Glicks** (`glicks.com.au`), who have been doing the best deli-style bagels this side of New York City since 1968. On the way, keep an eye out for the **Carlisle St Bridge**, which is marked with a sculpture monument of the 19th-century schooner *Lady of St Kilda*, a boat owned by one Sir Thomas Dyke Acland, and which sat moored offshore in these waters in 1842, from which the suburb took its name.

🡢 **NEARBY** Balaclava train station offers an out if you're done and dusted, but otherwise continue along Carlisle St to pass into **St Kilda East's** residential area. At Orrong Rd you'll take a left before turning right into Manor Grove to visit what is possibly Melbourne's most lavish mansion, the jaw-dropping **Labassa** (`nationaltrust.org.au/places/labassa`). Built in the 1880s, this Victoria-era French Renaissance mansion has 35 rooms, which, if you're lucky enough to be around on the third Sunday of the month, you can venture inside to discover the superb interior of stained glass windows and painted trompe l'oeil ceiling. Past residents include Australia's first Hollywood star Louis Lovely; when the building was subdivided into flats, it was a hippie hangout in the 1970s known for its cheap rent.

⚑ **THIS LAST LEG** takes you through to the well-heeled suburb of **Caulfield**, where young Bad Seeds Nick Cave, Mick Harvey, Phill Calvert and Tracey Pew were all schooled. Scoot on ahead along Balaclava Rd past Caulfield Park and racecourse, home to one of Australia's oldest and most famous horseraces, the **Caulfield Cup**, first run in 1879. When you reach Caulfield station, no doubt buggered, if somehow you have one more in you, the **Monash University Museum of Art** (monash.edu/muma) makes a fitting finish to this bohemian- and art-focused ride.

Local Chit-chat with Dave Graney

Dave Graney (davegraney.com), singer-songwriter for many bands since the late 1970s, including The Moodists, Dave Graney and Coral Snakes, Dave Graney and the Lurid Yellow Mist, and Dave Graney and the mistLY. He's the author of three books and you can also catch him on 3RRR (102.7) as host of Banana Lounge Broadcasting, Tuesdays, noon–2pm.

The Moodists played the legendary Crystal Ballroom back in the day; what are some of your memories?

It was run by Graeme Richmond, head of Richmond Football Club. We rehearsed there and had our dole cheques sent there. The downstairs bar was terrifying and full of tough guys. People lived in the George (Seaview Ballroom) and you could see them lounging on balconies from the street. It had a lovely staircase and a lift for the older residents. St Kilda was mainly full of interesting older people. It wasn't legendary at the time – it was just a great room, or several rooms. Beautifully dilapidated.

Likewise, the Prince of Wales and the Espy?

The Prince was lovely and seedy and once again rock music was just a small part of it. The biggest thing there was Pokies – a drag night. Pictures of the drag performers all up the stairs with short bios under each. The dressing room with old-school lights around the mirrors, racks of feather boas and dresses. We played in the piano bar upstairs on weeknights. People lived in the hotel. PBS 106.7 began there. Loved it. You parked on the roof and took your gear in . The Espy was always for blow-ins from the suburbs. Less of a hothouse creatively. Ran well in the late 80s, early 90s – a band would be paid $1200 to play in the front room. A nice earner.

What are some of the standout gigs you've seen in St Kilda over the years?

I am not really a punter. I liked playing shows there but I loved seeing Kim Salmon and the Surrealists rocking the Piano Bar in the Esplanade in about 1992. The Birthday Party were always great in the early 80s. St Kilda hasn't been any kind of rock capital since the late 90s. Music moved across the river and stayed. A pity but the bohemian culture was priced out.

What are some of the things that still make St Kilda great today?

Memo Music Hall is great. Readings Bookshop. The sea breeze and the sky.

CLICK, READ, LISTEN AND WATCH:

- stkildahistory.org.au
- Dolores San Miguel, *The Ballroom: The Melbourne Punk and Post-Punk Scene*
- Paul Kelly and the Coloured Girls, 'From St Kilda to Kings Cross'
- *Autoluminescent* (2011, directed by Richard Lowenstein and Lynn-Maree Milburn)
  Dogs in Space (1986, directed by Richard Lowenstein)

COLLINGWOOD & FITZROY

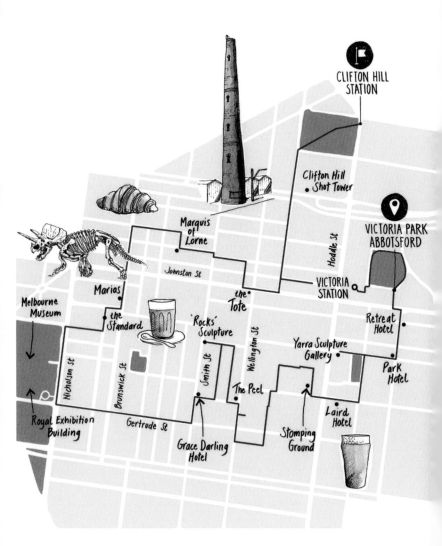

CLIFTON HILL
STATION

Clifton Hill
Shot Tower

Marquis
of
Lorne

Hoddle St

VICTORIA PARK
ABBOTSFORD

Johnston St

VICTORIA
STATION

Melbourne
Museum

Marios

the•
Tote

Retreat
Hotel

the
Standard

'Rocks'
Sculpture

Yarra Sculpture
Gallery

Park
Hotel

Nicholson st

Brunswick St

Smith St

Wellington St

The Peel

Royal Exhibition
Building

Gertrude St

Laird
Hotel

Grace Darling
Hotel

Stomping
Ground

START
Victoria Park, Abbotsford

FINISH
Clifton Hill station

DISTANCE
10km one-way

DURATION
Half- to full-day

TRANSPORT
If coming by train, arrive at Victoria Park station, and finish up at Clifton Hill station

CONNECTING RIDES
Capital City Trail (p28)
Main Yarra Trail
Merri Creek Trail (p84)

Taking in Melbourne's grungy inner north is this backstreet pedal through some of the city's coolest neighbourhoods. Visit Fitzroy's and Collingwood's hottest bars, cafes and restaurants (check opening hours and plan your ride accordingly), along with enchanting architecture and cutting-edge galleries. And take in Collingwood's colourful, chequered past in some of Melbourne's most infamous working-class streets.

UNLESS YOU'RE A ONE-EYED – and possibly missing-toothed – member of the Magpie Army, this is a route that starts deep among enemy lines: **Victoria Park**, spiritual home to the Collingwood Football Club. A ground where opposition teams, supporters and umpires (or white maggots as they're better known here) have all long feared to tread: from ice-cold showers in the visitor change rooms to a rabid local crowd baying for blood – sometimes taking things too far as happened with Nyoongar man and St Kilda footballer Nicky Winmar. In what's considered a watershed moment in sporting race relations, it was here in 1993 where Winmar famously stood up to racial abuse; to mark the 25-year anniversary, a statue of him was unveiled at Optus Stadium in Perth in 2019.

🚴 **CYCLING WITH KIDS:** Pack a footy and have a kick at **Victoria Park**. Stop at **Stomping Ground Brewery**, with its cubbie-house playground, and the oh-so-cute **Doll's House**. The **Store of Requirement** (thestoreofrequirement.com.au), has 'Butterbeer' for kids and other Harry Potter essentials. **Jasper Junior** (jasperjunior.com.au) in Smith St has quality traditional-style toys. Over Nicholson St, the **Melbourne Museum** and **IMAX** can keep you busy for a few hours.

📍 **WHERE YOU ROLL OFF THE PLATFORM** is actually Abbotsford, although it's the perfect place to begin a ride through both Collingwood and the gritty inner north as you start with a lap of the outside of the stadium. As you pass by its red-brick ticket booths and original signage, the past feels very much alive, and though the Pies haven't played here since 1999 (when the curtains were drawn on an illustrious 107 years of history), it's now home to a new era of footy: the women's league, where the black and white is represented in the AFLW. These days it's also a public park, so pop in to take a look inside the ground where you'll find info on its colourful history!

Long before grown men and women ran around here kicking a pigskin, this ground was covered in eucalyptus and casuarina trees, and was a place where grown men and women ran around kicking a possum skin! This here is the residing place of the Wurundjeri People, and at the south-east entrance there's a sculpture and tribute acknowledging them as the Traditional Owners, as well as references to Marngrook, the First Nations game pre-dating Australian Rules Football, where indeed possum-skin balls are believed to have be used.

➡️ **FROM THE FOOTY GROUND,** make your way along Rich St to hit busy Johnston St – watch out for the buses – and then turn right Nicholson St by the **Retreat Hotel** (retreatabbotsford.com.au). Dating back to 1873, this grand heritage-listed pub was the local watering hole on the 1970s and '80s TV drama *The Sullivans* and features an impressive Edwardian architectural design with turret tower, and a front bar that's just as elegant. Continue south along Nicholson St to another historical 19th-century backstreet boozer, **Park Hotel** (theparkhotel.com.au) where you'll turn right into Vere St. Among the cottages here it's comforting to find a few old-school dives in what's otherwise an area fast losing its original character to rapid-fire gentrification. Head into the railway underpass to find the **Yarra Sculpture Gallery** (yarrasculpturegallery.com.au), an artist-owned space set within an old whitewashed brick factory – it's worth parking the bike to check out exhibits of contemporary sculpture.

● **BACKTRACK AROUND** past the park to take a right along Park St to meet Gipps St, which leads on towards Hoddle St. Here's another historic pub, the **Laird** (`lairdhotel.com`), established back in 1847 and once an illegal gambling den frequented by the likes of Squizzy Taylor, one of Melbourne's notorious 1920s gangsters. These days it's known for a very different kind of scene, one involving anything from underwear parties to leather-themed nights for what's one of the area's longest-running gay bars. Across the way is **Collingwood Masonic Centre**, a handsome, heritage, brick building dating to 1928 and still owned by the Freemasons.

● **CROSS OVER** traffic-clogged Hoddle St to arrive in Collingwood proper, where you'll continue along Gipps St to take a sneaky right down the mural-decorated Islington St for a timely pit stop at **Stomping Ground** (`stompingground.beer`). Located within a converted warehouse, this popular local microbrewery features a cavernous, enclosed beer garden with retractable roof; there's a beer-friendly menu of pretzels, burgers and pizzas to enjoy with the 30 craft ales on tap.

● **PUSH ALONG** industrial Islington past the automotive workshops and panel beaters to stumble across an unexpected find, the delightful **Doll's House** – a tiny two-roomed heritage-listed cottage that pre-dated the concept of today's tiny house by about 150 years! From here you'll also spot **Collingwood Town Hall**, a colossal Victoria-era building and clock tower looming over Hoddle St.

● **MAKE YOUR WAY THROUGH** the adjoining carpark to ride past McCutcheon Way's murals and school gymnasium before turning left at **Campbell Rd**. Stop here to admire the wonderful 20-storey mural (the tallest in the southern hemisphere), the backdrop upon a canvas that is the beautified facade of high-rise housing commission flats. At Campbell Rd you'll ride among rows of cute heritage-listed 19th-century weatherboard houses, Collingwood's largest remnant of working-class housing and an area that in the 1880s had Melbourne's highest death rate due to its noxious trades.

⊖ **RETURNING TO** Gipps St, take a left at **Le Bon Ton** (`lebonton. com.au`), an attractive Edwardian hotel established in 1853 that was the former Glasshouse Hotel, named after the glass factory, Victoria's first, around the corner. In more recent times it's been Collingwood's preferred female same-sex bar, and though it still pulls a diverse crowd the main focus here is its delicious Louisiana-style American BBQ pit-smoked meats.

⊖ **HEAD BY** the old pub to cycle south along narrow Rokeby St and stop at the aforementioned Glasshouse Rd, where, as well the site of an old boot factory and tannery you'll find **Gertrude Glasshouse** (`gertrude.org.au`), one of many contemporary galleries in Collingwood and Fitzroy. Glasshouse Rd is one-way, so be careful.

⊖ **BACK ON** Rokeby St, continue along this industrial thoroughfare of warehouse design studios, fishmongers and more nefarious red-light establishments, to turn right into Northumberland St. At its far end is the red-brick, five-storey building that was the site of **Victoria Distillery** (c.1860), though today it's the site of an apartment complex. Back in the day, some 13,000 gallons (49,210 L) of gin and 7000 (26,500 L) of whisky were produced per week here! It was established by Thomas Aitken, who also set up the 1850s **Victoria Brewery** around the corner on Victoria Pde, a site famous for being the home of VB, the beer for a hard-earned thirst.

⊖ **AFTER TAKING A LOOK** at the edifice of the brewery (which is also now apartments), it's back northwards along Wellington St to duck into Brewery Lne to your right, at which point you're probably starting to catch on that booze is a theme of this trail! This is Collingwood after all, where pubs have always been an integral part of the suburb's identity. This one's another historic landmark, the **Yorkshire Brewery**, built in 1876 with its polychrome brick tower that's now surrounded by a new residential complex (relax, there are plenty of pubs coming up that aren't apartments!). There's some interesting info on the site to read before swinging round back on to Wellington to turn left at Peel St, which is famous for another gay Collingwood institution, the **Peel** (thepeel.com.au). Established in 1857 by the same owner as the brewery you just came from (John Wood), the Robert Peel Hotel features a towered heritage ornate facade and is one of oldest continuously trading pubs in Collingwood.

⊜ **RIDE ALONG** the plane tree–lined street and take a right at Cambridge St to ride by the old **Foy & Gibson** red-brick factories used to manufacture goods for the company's department store chain. Along here you'll find **Smith & Daughters** (smithanddaughters.com), Australia's first vegan restaurant to be awarded an acclaimed chef's hat. Along with its sit-down menu of creative mains, there's a deli offering more everyday (but no less inventive) sandwiches, toasties and cafe mains.

⊜ **AT THE END** of Cambridge St, take a left at Stanley St to head up the hill to the corner of Smith St where you'll see the **'Rocks' sculpture** by renowned public artist Glenn Romanis (glennromanis.com). This topographical sculpture uses inlaid stone to map local First Nations cultural sites of significance and is an important gathering place for local and visiting First Nations peoples to meet and unify.

⊜ **BEFORE** exploring Smith St properly, swing around back down the hill to turn right into Oxford St for what's an even more impressive display of Foy & Gibson warehouses, and where you'll be greeted by one of Collingwood's best cafes, **Proud Mary** (proudmarycoffee.com.au). A big player in Melbourne's third-wave coffee scene, this is the go-to place for quality single-origin beans and contemporary cafe fare.

Pepped up on caffeine, push off along Oxford's red-brick way to turn right into Peel St, and pass more historic sadly-no-more pubs to reach **Smith St.** Named by *Time Out* as the world's coolest street in 2021, this grungy strip is Melbourne's epicentre of diversity and alternative culture, luring musicians, artists, hipsters and students, among what's also now a pretty mainstream crowd, here for cool cafes, bars, cheap restaurants and record stores. It's a scene that all takes place among a strip of heritage buildings (with facades sporting signage from old piano makers and coffee palaces to Foy & Gibson department stores), most of which have been spruced up to become, sigh, you guessed it, more apartments...

⟫ **START AT** Collingwood's oldest pub (and Melbourne's second oldest), the bluestone **Grace Darling Hotel** (`thegracedarlinghotel.com.au`). Built in 1854, this gold-rush-era pub remains one of Smith St's best, both for its quality pub food and local drinks list, but also for its youthful rock'n'roll atmosphere with a bandroom upstairs offering gigs most nights. It's also the site where the Collingwood Football Club was formed in 1892.

⟫ **TAKE CARE NOT** to get skittled by the 86 tram as you proceed south along Smith St to turn right at Gertrude St to officially arrive in the suburb of **Fitzroy**, Melbourne's oldest suburb. Founded in 1839, it's another famed inner-city bohemian enclave and, like Collingwood, despite ongoing gentrification, it still attracts a creative, left-leaning crowd here for its edgy artsy and multicultural feel. On the corner is **Crumpler** (`crumpler.com/au`), a homegrown success story set up by two local bike-courier mates who conceived of a multimillion-dollar idea in the form of its iconic bike Messenger bag, designed to carry a slab of beer while cycling home from work! A quarter of a century later, and a dozen stores across the world, it's still here, and with the original owner back at the helm, teaming up with his daughter.

⟫ **CONTINUE WEST** along **Gertude St**, another Fitzroy institution where among vegetarian tacos, all-day breakfasts, record stores and iconic pubs like the **Builders Arms Hotel** (`buildersarmshotel.com.au`) you'll find more elegant offerings of wine bars, perfumeries, ceramics and designer boutiques. It's also an important area for Fitzroy and Collingwood's First Nations community, with many people moving here in the 1950s from missions across the state, many of whom were part of the Stolen Generations: the estimated one in three First Nations children who were removed from their families between 1910 and 1970 under official government policy. Among Fitzroy's parks and laneways, the **Atherton Gardens** here on the corner of Gertrude and Napier sts was the most well-known gathering place for people looking for family, including local and ARIA Hall of Famer Archie Roach, whose album *Charcoal Lane* (1990) was inspired by the very area you now stand in. Within the gates of the commission flats is a **tribute to the Stolen Generations** by First Nations artist Reko Rennie, with his work *Remember Me* featuring spears, coolamon (traditional carrying vessel) and boomerang-shaped seating. These streets are also home to organisations such as the Victorian Aboriginal Health Service and the Aboriginal Community Youth Club Gymnasium, where historical plaques mark the spot of notable places such as the Koori Club at 43 Gertrude St (now a sake bar), an 'Aboriginal Only' club for young Black Power activists to gather – a scene that drew Muhammad Ali here for a visit in 1979. Around here marks the halfway point in today's ride, so if you want a quick refreshment, Gertude St's a good place to find one.

⊙ **AHEAD LIES** Fitzroy's celebrated Brunswick St, which we'll keep for later on, but in the meantime shift your attention to the left, where at number 7 Brunswick St is the birthplace of Australia's only saint, **Mary MacKillop**. If you'd like to know more about her fascinating life, the **Mary MacKillop Heritage Centre** (`mmhc.org.au`) has a museum devoted to her a few blocks away in East Melbourne.

⊙ **IN THE MEANTIME** keep on cycling along Gertrude to reach Nicholson St where on the corner you'll pass the Italianate 19th-century former **cable tram engine house** to cross over at the lights for a brief rendezvous with **Carlton**. Here at the gardens is a sprawling **Moreton Bay Fig** that during the 1920s and '40s was an important gathering area for First Nations activists to speak out on injustices. And that little building to your right? That's the World Heritage-listed **Royal Exhibition Building** (`museumsvictoria.com.au/reb`) a spectacular building dating from 1880 that takes in a mix of Italian Renaissance, Byzantine, Romanesque and Lombardic architectural styles; if you're around at 2pm you can join a daily tour to see its equally stunning interior. Further along is the **Melbourne Museum** (`museumsvictoria.com.au`). If you have time to duck in to see one thing, make it the **Bunjilaka Aboriginal Cultural Centre**, which does a wonderful job in telling the stories of the First Nations peoples of Victoria. Phar Lap and the ginormous skeleton of a blue whale are other museum highlights. An equally impressive bunch of bones – a Triceratops's fossilised skeleton – has just arrived, but tickets are needed to see it.

⊘ **MAKE YOUR WAY ALONG** Nicholson to cross back over to Fitzroy at the lights, taking note of the three-storey brick **Nunnery** (`nunnery.com.au`) built in 1888, and now a popular guesthouse. Duck into classy Moor St with its Victorian terraces and cross over Fitzroy St where to your left is the classic **Standard Hotel** (`thestandardhotel.com.au`), many a local's favourite for Fitzroy's best backstreet pub (notable mentions also go out to the Rose, the Napier and the Union Club Hotel). Pedal on to hit gritty **Brunswick St**, one of Melbourne's best nightlife, shopping and dining precincts. Here you'll be smashed for choice with the many historic pubs, cool bars, vegan cafes, cheap Vietnamese restaurants, art galleries, vintage clothing, second-hand bookstores, cocktail bars, band venues and a billion souvlaki shops for that all-important 2am last port of call. But if that all sounds too hectic for a bike ride, you can always stick to the side streets, or better yet, lock up the bike and go for a stroll along this pulsating thoroughfare. If you're looking for somewhere quintessentially Fitzroy, it's hard to go past **Marios** (`marioscafe.com.au`), a retro Italian cafe that's been serving up a classic menu of traditional pastas and bistro mains, along with breakfasts, cakes and, of course, espresso since 1986.

⊘ **FURTHER AHEAD** is Rose St, which hosts the weekend **art market** (`rosestmarket.com.au`); where it runs across Brunswick St, you'll find Melbourne's best croissants at **Lune Croissanterie** (`lunecroissanterie.com`). Continue east past Rose St's historic buildings to take a right into George St to pass another hidden Fitzroy icon, the 1873 **Marquis of Lorne** (`www.marquisoflorne.com.au`) another old-school pub refurbed with modern-day flair and where across the road is the **Centre for Contemporary Photography** (CCP; `ccp.org.au`), always worth dropping by for its quality exhibitions.

➡ **IT'S THEN** back over Smith St to return to Collingwood where this side of Johnston you'll again be spoilt for choice with taqueiras (`tortasandtacos.com.au`), IPA-dedicated brewpubs (`fixationbrewing.com.au`) and microbreweries (`themillbrewery.com.au`), craft gin distilleries (`thecraftandco.com.au`) and coffee roasters (`everyday-coffee.com`), along with an entire strip of retail outlets offering bargains galore. But if you've got burgers on your mind, it's an easy choice: head down Easey St for kick-ass cheeseburgers at **Easey's** (`easeys.com.au`) in a unique setting of old-school Met trains that are plonked on top of rooftop like an audacious art sculpture. Easey St is also home to one of Melbourne's most grisly crime scenes, when back in 1977 two women were brutally murdered in their home, a case, known as the Easey St murders, that remains unsolved today.

➡ **TAKE A RIGHT** into Budd St to cross over Johnston to check out the art precinct at **Collingwood Yards** (`collingwoodyards.org`) with its studios, galleries, rooftop bar and coffee shop set up in what was the former Collingwood Technical School. Next door, admire the **Keith Haring mural** (`melbourneharingmural.com.au`), a wonderful gift left behind by the famous New York street artist who dropped by in 1984 to paint this piece.

➡ **A FEW DOORS UP** is the **Tote** (`thetotehotel.com`), Melbourne's famed sticky-carpet rock'n'roll venue so cherished that its threatened closure became an all-important election issue that shaped the 2010 state election. But before there was *the* Tote, there was another Tote – a totalisator or machine for pooling bets and calculating winnings proportionately – owned by John Wren, a legendary Collingwood identity, who ran this venue up the road at 148 Johnston as an illegal gambling den. Hidden behind the facade of a tobacconist and tea shop, it was immortalised in Frank Hardy's *Power without Glory*, and today is marked by a heritage plaque.

➡ **SWING BACK** into Johnston to head north into Gold St where you'll take a right at the roundabout for a quick look at a house with a difference, a pre-fabricated cottage imported here from Singapore during the gold rush at **136 Sackville St**.

🚩 **BACK ON** Gold St, cycle along for four blocks to cross over Hotham to reach **Goldy's! Tavern** (goldystavern.com.au), the former Leinster Arms Hotel that's since been revitalised under its new owners. Many remember it as the local haunt of another infamous Collingwood identity, Chopper Read, a well-known criminal (whom Eric Bana played in cult-classic *Chopper*). As a 17-year-old Read murdered union boss heavyweight Desmond Costello outside this pub in 1971 before dumping his body at the nearby **Clifton Hill Shot Tower**, which is your next stop. This 80m tall heritage-listed shot tower (the world's tallest) was built in 1882 and is reached by cycling north over Alexander Pde to reach Clifton Hill. Here you'll continue along Gold St and cut through Darling Gardens to cross Hoddle St and make your way along John St to Clifton Hill station to complete what hopefully has given you a good taste of why these inner-north suburbs are among Melbourne's most cherished.

Local Chit-chat with Tahnee Edwards

Gammin Threads (gamminthreads.com) is the creative outlet for Yorta Yorta and Taungurung woman Tahnee Edwards. Inspired by her love of culture, community and cool aunties, Tahnee's use of bold colours, humour and messages that speak to issues that impact community mean Gammin Threads represents much more than just clothing. It speaks to pride, women's empowerment and community, and credits the Blak Matriarchy as the backbone of community.

Tell us a little about Gammin Threads and how it all came about?

I studied graphic design and fashion merchandising at uni, then after working in fashion for a year, I started working in community at Djirra (djirra.org.au), an organisation that supports Aboriginal women who have experienced family violence. I was going through a big creative block as my mum was terminally ill, and, as much as I wanted to get back into fashion, I really loved working in community: I was around all these strong Aboriginal women, I felt supported, and I was just finally doing work that I felt proud of. Then in 2018 something just sort-of shifted; the NAIDOC theme was 'Because of her, we can' and the work we were doing at Djirra inspired me to make these designs around the matriarchy and respecting women. I didn't realise at the time that this would become my little label/business. But this is the kind of fashion I've always loved – streetwear with slogans, graphic tees; this is what I've always wanted to do.

Your father, Uncle Talgium Edwards, grew up in Fitzroy/ Collingwood so that must've been cool to collaborate with him on an art project that was nominated for the Best in Visual Arts Awards as part of the 2019 Deadly Fringe in Melbourne.

Whenever I came to Melbourne to visit Dad I would always be hanging out on Brunswick St or Smith St. I grew up in a small country town, so there was nothing like it back home. I loved it; it's creative and inspiring and I love the history. I have a studio in Fitzroy with my friend who's also a blackfella in business: Kristy from Haus of Dizzy. It's such a cool space; 15-year-old Tahnee would be so proud and psyched to see it. But I was given the opportunity to have an exhibition (*Edwards Gammin Café*) at SEVENTH gallery on Gertrude St for Deadly Fringe in 2019.

My Dad's experience of Fitzroy and Gertrude St in the '70s is completely different to my version today. I thought nothing suits gentrified Fitzroy more than a hipster cafe, serving up a Blak-themed menu and little Blak references throughout.

CLICK, READ, LISTEN AND WATCH:

- 🌐 collingwoodhs.org.au
  aboriginalhistoryofyarra.com.au
  fitzroyhistorysociety.org.au
- 📖 Tony Birch, *Shadowboxing*
  Helen Garner, *Monkey Grip*
  Frank Hardy, *Power without Glory*
  Chopper Read, *Chopper: From the Inside*
  Peter Rose, *Rose Boys*
  Helen Thomas, *Murder on Easey Street*
- 🎵 Dan Sultan, 'Old Fitzroy'
  Archie Roach, *Charcoal Lane*
- 🎬 *The Club* (1980, directed by Bruce Beresford)

NORTHSIDE

Oakover Rd

Pastor Sir Doug Nicholls Oval

Croxton

Thornbury Picture House

Fitzroy Stars

Welcome to THORNBURY

Welcome to Thornbury

St Georges Rd

High St

NORTHCOTE STATION

Northcote Social Club

Wesley Anne

Northcote Theatre

Northcote Town Hall

Clarke St

Merri Creek

Palace Westgarth Cinema

Westgarth St

Edinburgh Gardens

Hoddle St

CLIFTON HILL STATION

START
Northcote

FINISH
Clifton Hill

DISTANCE
12.5km one-way

DURATION
half- to full-day

TRANSPORT
Northcote train station makes for a convenient arrival point to explore these streets in a loop that finishes up at Clifton Hill station

CONNECTING RIDES
Capital City Trail (p28)
Merri Creek Trail (p84)
Northern Pipe Trail
Western Ring Road Trail

This ride leads you into the heart of Melbourne's cool northern 'burbs on a day exploring its string of neighbourhood cafes, restaurants, bars and band venues. It's a route mixing lively thoroughfares lined with grand architecture with relaxed backstreets and dedicated bike trails.

WHEN IT COMES to Melbourne's inner north, Fitzroy, Collingwood and Carlton have long been considered the coolest and most interesting places to live. And that's all good if you've got a spare couple of mil to drop on a tiny house or apartment, to go with the exorbitant rent, but what happens to all the artists, musicians, writers, students, dropouts and originals who can no longer afford to live here? Well, they move on to the suburbs further out to build their own new little creative scene, before they're priced out of that one! And that's where we're riding today, through the City of Darebin, to check out the new guard of Melbourne's northside, visiting places like Northcote, Thornbury and Preston.

🚲 CYCLING WITH KIDS: High St is busy, so consider using the side streets between places like **Big Dreams** (bigdreams.com.au) toy shop and **Keke and Kaka** (kekeandkaka.com.au), Japanese toys and gifts. Eat anything from ramen and pizza to cookies (thecookiedoughco.com.au) and gelato (Lipari Gelato Bar) – or take in a **movie** (Westgarth or Thornbury). Kick a footy at **Sir Douglas Nicholls Oval**. And the Art Deco architectural gem on Queens Parade happens to be home to the golden arches...

📍 **NORTHCOTE STATION IS WHERE WE BEGIN.** This suburb is knocking on the door of that aforementioned list of where everyone wants to live. So much so, in fact, that it took out the number one spot in Pricewaterhouse Cooper's 2021 poll on Melbourne's best places to live. It's a neighbourhood of attractive houses and stately architecture to go with bespoke cafes, restaurants and bars that cater to your more refined, left-leaning, fedora-wearing set.

➡️ **AT THE TRAIN STATION** take a left to ride along Herbert St for a little warm-up lap of these backstreets as you pop into the Herbert Cafe (theherbert.com.au) for a well-made coffee and gourmet vegetarian toasties in a space that was a former mechanic. At the corner, take a right into Arthurton St for 100m, looking out for traffic along this busy narrow thoroughfare, before wheeling over to cross at Helen St. Along here you'll pass a series of cute 19th-century terraces, where workers from the slaughter yards or clay pits once lived. Further along you'll find an antique furniture shop that's moved into an old-red brick warehouse, where, just before you reach Northcote Primary School (c. 1880s), it becomes a one-way street. Abiding by the road rules, dismount to briefly walk your bike to turn left into Hawthorn Rd to hit High St, one of Melbourne's most vibrant shopping streets where it's all about eating, drinking and boutiques, and where a young Queen Elizabeth II and Prince Philip visited back in 1954 as part of their royal procession, the first ever visit by a reigning monarch.

➡️ **ON THE CORNER** is the **Northcote Social Club** (NSC; northcotesocialclub.com), a pub and band room that brings a healthy dose of rock'n'roll to what's otherwise more of an indie-chic kinda vibe. The NSC has hosted the likes of the Pixies to Paul Kelly (as well Lady Ga Ga's post-gig after-party!); at other times you can stop by for a parma and a pot in a hotel that originally dates back to the 1850s.

⊙ **FROM HERE** you'll cross at the lights and turn right to ride south along High St; it's a bustling thoroughfare, so take it slow and stick to the bike lane. Otherwise feel free to walk your bike along the pavement as there's plenty to see among these 19th-century shopfronts housing local fashion labels, bookstores, vinyl shops, vintage clothing, pizza spots and Vietnamese restaurants, along with cool cafes and bars. The **Wesley Anne** (`wesleyanne.com.au`) is your classic Northcote venue and long one of its most popular spots for a drink and a meal with a show (mainly folksy, jazz kinda bands) in an atmospheric back room set inside a former church dating to 1859.

If you have any doubts as to whether Melbourne really is the world's live-music capital, then the brand new 1500-seater **Northcote Theatre** (`northcotetheatre.com`) should dispel any uncertainty. And when we say 'new' it's anything but; instead it's a grand Edwardian Baroque building dating to 1912 and is the oldest purpose-built picture theatre in Victoria (and possibly Australia). After closing in the 1960s, it served as a reception centre before reopening in 2022 as a regal auditorium not just for international and local gigs but also as a mezzanine wine bar, Italian restaurant and rooftop cocktail bar.

⊙ **MAKING YOUR WAY UP** the gradual ascent, you'll ride by one of Northcote's oldest pubs, the **Peacock Hotel** (`peacockinnhotel.com`), a gastro/sports pub that dates to 1854 and is heritage-listed for its 1930s Egyptian/Deco-styled facade. Reaching the top of Ruckers Hill, you can't miss the majestic **Northcote Town Hall**, but we're going to leave this for a closer inspection on the way back. Instead, it's a roll down along the other side of Ruckers Hill, where things open up as you glide down the red-brick bridge as the city skyline appears ahead in the distance.

HIGH ST MORPHS INTO the little village suburb of Westgarth at this point, with more cafes, boutiques and bars. There's plenty to like here, including **Merri Creek Tavern** (`facebook.com/111HighStreet`) a little rock'n'roll bar with vinyl and live bands; ambient and intimate **Kelvin Bar** (`instagram.com/kelvinbarofficial_butlaidback`) that's clocked up more than 25 years here; and **Barry** (`facebook.com/barrycoffeeandfood`) a cafe for contemporary brunches and great coffee. But it's the **Palace Westgarth Cinema** (`palacecinemas.com.au/cinemas/palace-westgarth`) that this area is best known for: a beautiful Art Deco landmark dating to 1921 and featuring an interior just as splendid.

HERE YOU'LL SAY GOODBYE to High St (for the moment, anyway) and turn left into Westgarth St for a short ride, before taking another left into South Cres to curve around Westgarth station. Now we explore Northcote's residential streets with their mix of Victorian terraces, California bungalows and Edwardian weatherboards. And there's another type of house here too, one so familiarly suburban it's easily overlooked. It's the distinctive red-brick veneer houses built by the Greek and Italian postwar immigrants. With their decorative colonnades, lion statuettes and concrete front gardens, admittedly they're no oil paintings, but they're a very northern suburbs–style of home that, perhaps one day, might get heritage overlays like the others in the street.

FROM SOUTH CRES, take a left into Mason St to find another celebrated part of Melbourne's suburbia – the humble milk bar. This one, like most others 'round here, has been converted into a cafe, **South Crescent Cafe** (`facebook.com/southcrescentcafe`), which makes a relaxed stop for quality coffee and all your smashed avo needs.

➲ **RIDE ALONG** Mason St for a couple of blocks before turning left into Clarke St to continue this architectural tour, with a stunning succession of heritage mansions as well as a block of two-storey Victorian terraces (186–192 Clarke St) built by the owner so he could look out over the harness-racing track at the trots that used to be held below Ruckers Hill.

➲ **IT'S THEN UP THE HILL** to turn right back on to High St's Ruckers Hill for the most resplendent building of them all, the Northcote Town Hall with its grand Neoclassical facade dating to 1891.Today it's an integral part of Darebin's vibrant arts scene with a quality program of gigs and performances put on by the **Northcote Town Hall Arts Centre** (facebook.com/northcotetownhallartscentre). If someone's around you can take a look at its Art Deco main hall.

Otherwise be sure to head next door to the adjoining Civic Square, which is decorated with First Nations murals and motifs by Gunnai artist Ray Thomas. Long before anyone named Rucker built his mansion on top of this hill (which incidentally was on the corner of High and Bayview sts and demolished in the 1925), this area was well known as a spot the Wurundjeri People (the Traditional Owners of this land) would gather for ceremonies and corroborees.

➲ **ALONGSIDE** the town hall on the other side is another grand Neoclassical building in the **old Northcote Carnegie Library**, gifted to the city by American philanthropist Andrew Carnegie in 1911, the same one who built Carnegie Hall in New York.

➲ **CONTINUE DOWN** the other side of High St, where you'll find notable stops include **Joe's Shoestore** (joesshoestore.com.au), a hip bar open from 5pm for a post-ride tipple, vinyl and gourmet pizzas in a place that, you guessed it, was a former shoe store owned by a guy named Joe. And few doors up is Northcote's finest restaurant, **Estelle** (theestelle.com.au), one that's worth bringing a spare set of fancy clothes for, for its set-menu dinners or Sunday roast lunches that you'll need to pre-book.

⊙ **THEN IT'S BACK PAST** the NSC to continue along High St, with a delicious choice of multicultural offerings of everything from ramen and dumplings to vegan Vietnamese (`brotherbon.com.au`) and Tibetan momos (`wildyakrestaurant.com`).

⊙ **ONCE YOU CROSS OVER** Separation St it's a less grand affair with fairly uninspired new developments of apartments and office spaces, but plenty of restaurants and cafes to choose from. Among it all there's a bit of history, including McLean's tannery (486–494 High St) that used to stink out these suburbs during a north wind; an ironmonger in a building (468 High St) still there and now a great cafe doing all-day brunches (`fieldblack.com.au`); and further afield **Northcote Soldiers and Sailors Memorial Hall** (496 High St) built in 1922 for the 2000 or so soldiers from Northcote who served in World War I.

⊙ **A FEW DOORS UP** it's time to say **Welcome to Thornbury** (`welcometothornbury.com`); well not quite, it's still actually Northcote, but this outdoor playground for hipsters (if they're still a thing) is where you'll find food trucks and quality drinks set inside a former Morris Minor factory.

⊙ **AHEAD** is the **Croxton** (`croxtonparkhotel.com.au`), a historic pub (est. 1844) that's long been an confounding venue; it's a mishmash of heritage building with modern-day eyesore architecture, and serves as a dodgy pokies pub as well as a legendary rock'n'roll venue (hosting everyone from ACDC and INXS to Sleaford Mods and Jesus & Mary Chain). But whatever it is, they don't make places like this any more!

Other places along here include the **Thornbury Local** (`thethornburylocal.com`) a neighbourhood bar with an American menu of buffalo wings and po'boys among other American dishes; **Cactus Room** (`cactusroom.com.au`) for local alternative bands and exhibitions; **Franklin's Bar** (franklinsbar.com) a cool converted warehouse slinging up great drinks with nightly DJs; and **Cafe Gummo** (cafegummo.com) a divey underground hangout for the local youngsters in the know.

⊘ **PEDAL ALONG** past the old **Salvation Army Hall** (c. 1914) and **Northern Git** (getatgit.com), which has a menu of modern British, before reaching the old-school Thornbury classic **Monticello Cakes & Continental Gelati** that's been piping fresh ricotta cannoli since 1967. A few doors along is another original, the **Thornbury Theatre** (thethornburytheatre.com), back then the Regent Theatre, a regal 1920s picture house that's so old it was built during the time of silent films (*Argentine Love* was the first movie shown here accompanied by the Regent Grand Symphony Orchestra). Today it's a well-respected live-music venue hosting weekend gigs by quality Australian and international bands. Other times you'll find the **Thornbury Taphouse** (thornburytaphouse.com) with a rotating beer selection and decent food.

And while the grand old theatre may not have screened movies since the 1960s, across the road **Thornbury Picture House** (thornburypicturehouse.com.au) has stepped up to fill the void. This retro family-owned cinema screens new releases and cult classics in an Art Deco building (c. 1920) that was once an old drive-through petrol station. There are a few more places to keep an eye out for here: **All Are Welcome Thornbury** (all-are-welcome.com), an offshoot of their Northcote bakery, for pork-and-fennel sausage rolls, croissants and coffee; **Joanie's Baretto** (joaniesbaretto.com.au) for wonderful Italian bar snacks, pastas and aperitivi that goes hand in hand with its sister restaurant **Umberto Espresso Bar** (umberto.com.au) for a similar deal but open for lunch. And in between the two is **Ice-cream Social** (icecreamsocial.com.au) for seasonal experimental flavours, from miso and walnut to gin garden sorbet; don't overlook Portuguese tarts across the road at **Casa Nata** (casanata.com.au).

CROSSING OVER Miller St, the road splits into two, so stick to the left and remain on High St as you arrive in Preston. Opposite the heritage-listed Junction Hotel (c. 1859) is the **Gertrude Contemporary** (gertrude.org.au), a fantastic gallery that relocated here a few years ago from Fitzroy, just like many of the local residents. After one block, turn left into Oakover Rd to pass the reception centre for what's a pretty industrial stretch over the train lines that leads to St Georges Rd. At its end you'll link up with the Northern Pipe Trail, a dedicated bike track that runs from Reservoir station to Merri Creek. But today we're riding its southern section, aka the **St Georges Bike Path**.

TURN LEFT at St Georges Rd; the trail starts along the footpath where you'll ride by the New Preston Depot for a behind-the-scenes look at the engine room that keeps Melbourne's vast tram network a well-oiled machine – a sentiment perhaps not all commuters will agree with!

AT THE LIGHTS you'll cross over to reach a series of moving murals depicting local First Nations cultures put together by artists in consultation with people of the Kulin Nation. The first comprises a collage of paintings by William Barak, a well-respected Wurundjeri leader, who as well a tireless campaigner for First Nations rights was a talented painter, with his works originally painted in ochre and charcoal. The second mural features the disturbing imagery of two men from the Kimberley region shackled in chains, bringing light to the tragedy of dispossession and massacres that took place across both Victoria and Australia. The other murals explore struggles for land rights and a celebration of notable First Nations people, including world champion boxer Lionel Rose, Eddie Koiki Mabo (who led the landmark Native Title claim in the High Court, which overruled the legal fiction of terra nullius just six months after his death in 1992), and Sir Doug Nicholls and his wife, Lady Gladys, which leads in to our next stop: the **Pastor Sir Doug Nicholls Oval.**

⊖ **FROM THE MURALS**, the St Georges Bike Path heads down the median strip beside the tram line, where you'll take a left into Watt St to pass alongside the footy ground that's home to the **Fitzroy Stars** (fitzroystars.com.au). This predominantly First Nations football team was established in 1973 and currently plays in the Northern Football League. The ground is named after Sir Douglas Nicholls (1906–1988), a Yorta Yorta man born in the Cummeragunja Reserve, NSW, who lived a remarkable life. As well as playing footy for Northcote in the VFA, he played 54 games for Fitzroy in the VFL, and became the first First Nations player to pull on the 'Big V' in interstate footy before poor eye sight cut short his career. He was also the first First Nations person to become knighted, and went on to become a respected pastor and the governor of South Australia. But he was best known for his advocacy for social justice in First Nations rights, and helped to set up the Aboriginal Advancement League (aal.org.au) that's based here today. Riding along Watts St you'll encounter more stunning murals featuring notable First Nations individuals decorating the AAL's outer walls.

⊖ **ONCE YOU'VE TAKEN A LOOK AROUND**, head back down Watts St to rejoin the palm-lined bike trail through the other end of Thornbury and Northcote. At Batman Park (which the Darebin City Council is still in talks to rename as something more culturally sensitive to First Nations peoples), you'll be treated to wonderful city views. The dedicated trail continues on for another 1km till you reach the junction at St Georges Rd and Merri Parade, where you'll cross at the lights and veer to the right to continue along St Georges Rd. Here you'll spot a bike repair station, which marks the path for **Merri Creek Trail** (p84) down to the left. Stick to the main road to cross the bridge over the creek as you head into North Fitzroy, a suburb that's like a more relaxed, older hippy sibling of Fitzroy with lovely heritage buildings, cool neighbourhood pubs, cafes and restaurants.

Danny's Burgers (facebook.com/Dannysburgs) up the road gets many locals' vote for Melbourne's best burger. It's been flipping since 1945 and, with its 3am closing time, it's catered to many generations of late-night drunken revellers stumbling home. Crossing over Holden St, ride by the Neoclassical three-storey former hotel (c. 1889) to ride on to Park St, where you'll cross over the former Inner Circle railway line, now part of the **Capital City Trail** (p28). Further up you'll see the ornate **Pinnacle Hotel** (fitzroypinnacle.com.au) a superb historic building (c. 1888) that was a former post office. At Scotchmer St cross to the other side of St Georges Rd to find an Art Deco building that houses Aboriginal Housing Victoria, who assist with affordable housing for First Nations peoples. Crossing again at the lights, you'll reach what is arguably North Fitzroy's most well-known local landmark, **Piedimonte's Supermarket** (piedimonte.com.au), an Italian-owned business since 1958, where you can pop in to pick up some delicious produce for a picnic for the next stop at Edinburgh Gardens, further along St Georges Rd.

Here take note of the old gas lamps before riding along a stretch known to foodies for the hatted restaurants **Ryne** (ryne.com.au) for modern French fine dining, and **Horn Please** (hornplease.com.au) one of Melbourne's best for creative Indian street food. Where St Georges Rd turns into Brunswick St (p153), a ride for another day, we take a left to ride through the heritage-listed **Edinburgh Gardens**. Park the bike and take a breather to enjoy a picnic or read a book or just stare up at the clouds. Adjoining the park is the old Brunswick St Oval, a former VFL ground where Fitzroy used to play up until 1966.

➲ **ONCE YOU'RE DONE RELAXING**, head through to the other side to circle around Alfred Cres to admire some of the inner north's most stately mansions that overlook the gardens. Turn into Rowe St, a wide residential side street with a classic North Fitzroy feel, for a few blocks before turning right into Rushall Cres to zip through the roundabout to meet the major thoroughfare of Queens Pde at Clifton Hill. Here you'll find Melbourne's most stunning Art Deco building, and what is it? A McDonald's, of all things! Originally it was the United Kingdom Hotel, built back in 1938. Head 'round the side to Dummet Cres and take a tunnel underpass to find your way into Hoddle St.

This is where one of Melbourne's most tragic crimes took place back in 1987 when 26 people were shot: an event known as the Hoddle St massacre, which resulted in the death of nine people.

⚑ **THERE'S NOWHERE TO CROSS OVER** at Hoddle St, so stick to the footpath until you get to the lights at Ramsden St where you'll make your way over to John St to loop back around to reach Clifton Hill station. This completes your ride through Melbourne's northside suburbs.

Local Chit-chat with Nathan Muller

Nathan Muller, owner of Wesley Anne.

How did the Wesley Anne come about, and how has the place evolved over the years?

It was originally built as a Wesleyan Methodist church in 1854. Back then a church was more than just a church. It was also a school, a place where people congregated and came for all kinds of meetings. Before we took it over it in 2003, it was anything from a council chamber to an auction house and a bar and grill. At the time in Northcote, there wasn't much going on. Most of the shops had 'For Lease' signs on them and you could park a semitrailer down the street with ease all while seeing tumbleweeds blowing down the street. Since then the place has ebbed and flowed to cater to different crowds but our main focus here at Wesley Anne is to try to keep the place small and consistent for emerging artists. And the more established artists who do play here understand it's not necessarily about dominating the space but more so contributing to the atmosphere. The band room has always been a classic venue for an album launch or someone who's just finding their feet in the industry.

What makes the place different to your usual bar and band venue?

The personnel, I think. As well as the people who come here, our staff who work here exude their personality on the place. And with the music and food, it all comes together to make it an enjoyable experience for all.

What's Wesley Anne like during the day?

As well as a lunch service, you'll get casual lounge-y sort of vibe, but with its beautiful tree-filled courtyard out the back it offers you a refuge from the street.

What do you love about the Northcote area?

Around this area you'll find a pretty good level of diversity, so there's a lot of genuine people. And a lot of people who've lived in the area a long time, so it's a very community-minded place. It's one of those areas – particularly on a Thursday to Sunday – where if you wander up and down the street and can find a little bit of everything. There might be a choir singing across the road in the church, there might be a high-profile band playing down at the Northcote Social Club, a football match or other sports up on the big-screen at the Peacock, or just stopping in for a pleasant glass of wine at the Wesley Anne to watch the world go by.

CLICK, READ, LISTEN AND WATCH:

🌐 heritage.darebinlibraries.vic.gov.au

🎵 The Bedroom Philosopher, 'Northcote (So Hangover)'
Courtney Barnett, 'Depreston'
The Lucksmiths, 'Under The Rotunda'

🎞 *The Fitzroy Stars* (2008), directed by Daniel King and John Harding

DAYTRIPS AND

REGIONAL RIDES

BELLARINE RAIL TRAIL

SOUTH GEELONG STATION

Great Ocean Road Brewing

Moolap Train Station

Curlewis Golf Club

Drysdale

Portarlington Rd

Queenscliff Rd

GMHBA Stadium

Geelong Showgrounds

Bellarine Hwy

Leura Park Estate

Lonsdale Tomato Farm

QUEENSCLIFF STATION

Swan Island

Suma Park Railway

Swan Bay

Point Lonsdale

START
South Geelong station

FINISH
Queenscliff station

DISTANCE
36km one-way

DURATION
6–8 hours return

TRANSPORT
Take either the ferry from the Docklands or the V-line train from Melbourne's Southern Cross station to arrive at South Geelong station. Alternatively you can arrive from Sorrento by taking the ferry to Queenscliff to do the ride in the opposite direction.

CONNECTING RIDES
Barwon River Trail
Bay Trail (p40)

Offering the perfect escape for city-dwellers seeking a coastal adventure and some fresh country air, the Bellarine Rail Trail is one of regional Victoria's most accessible rail trails: a peaceful ride that traces the historical Geelong-Queenscliff railway line through picturesque farmland to arrive at the heritage seaside town of Queenscliff.

THERE ARE A LOT of reasons to love the Bellarine Peninsula – the beaches, the wineries, the relaxed coastal towns – but the drive here is definitely not one. In fact, it's probably the most boring drive there is: a featureless road with such a dearth of things to see that even playing 'I spy' will challenge beyond P for paddocks and H for hoon. Fortunately you don't need to worry about that as you'll be arriving via train or ferry before you hit the Bellarine Rail Trail, where all of a sudden the journey here becomes *the* reason to visit!

🚲 **CYCLING WITH KIDS: Curlewis Golf Club** has a tasty kids' menu and mini golf. This is a long ride, so we suggest visiting on a weekend (or school holidays) so you can hitch a ride on the historic steam train from Drysdale to Queenscliff, where there's plenty to do, including the **Queenscliff Fort** and the fascinating **Maritime Museum**.

SPEEDING ACROSS the bay in a purpose-built catamaran ferry makes for a pretty memorable first leg as you wheel your bike on to the Geelong Flyer (`portphillipferries.com.au`) at the Docklands' terminal. The train from Southern Cross is also a leisurely way to arrive; it'll take you directly to South Geelong station, in keeping with the day's theme – one that follows the old rail line from Geelong to Queenscliff. Opening in 1879, it was in operation for almost 100 years till its closure in 1976, and was used to carry passengers, local salt workers and defence staff back and forth from Fort Queenscliff.

The landscapes you'll pass are those of the Wathaurong People, the Traditional Owners who have resided here for over 25,000 years. William Buckley, the escaped convict, famously spent 32 years living among them from 1803, and his story of that time is a fascinating insight into the Wathaurong culture and way of life.

BEGINNING FROM SOUTH GEELONG STATION you'll disembark to the backdrop of Geelong's AFL stadium – known as the Cattery in footy circles – where players nicknamed the likes of God and Buddha graced the ground: it's much very hallowed turf out this way! The path is well signed from the moment you roll off the platform, starting out from the far end as you're led through South Geelong's industrial backstreets. Out here may not be an oil painting, but one sight for sore eyes is **Great Ocean Road Brewing** (`facebook.com/greatoceanroadbrewing`), a quality local microbrewery that opens up on Friday and Saturday afternoons and provides a great option to stop off on your return journey.

LOOK OUT for trucks and the local G-town revheads as you navigate the suburb of Breakwater's busy roundabout (while sticking to the shared pedestrian–cycle sidewalk), where you'll leave the train line to pass the Geelong Showgrounds. From here you'll coast through nondescript residential areas of Thompson and Newcomb before finding yourself among horse paddocks as you breathe a sigh of relief to leave Geelong's suburbia behind. Cross the Bellarine Highway at the pedestrian lights to arrive in Moolap, where a drive-in coffee joint awaits if you're seeking a caffeine hit.

● **AHEAD** lies the first proper stop at the old **Moolap train station** where a shelter and information board details not just its history (which dates to 1881) but its remnant native grasslands that made up part of this volcanic plain. Continuing on, you'll notice that things soon become very rural as suddenly cows and horses outnumber houses as the trail continues its way through Leopold's farmland and woodland reserves to cross Melaluka Rd, where Leopold train station remains in name only after its station building was destroyed by a storm in 1948. You'll see new housing estates – which are popping up across all of Greater Geelong and the Bellarine – at which point you'll reach a gentle incline that'll have you puffing along in second gear.

● **PASSING THROUGH** farmland, along the clearing to your left, you'll see the You Yangs looming in the distance – a significant cultural site and gathering place for the Wathaurong People. Further along is the old **Curlewis station** with a rest shelter, local history and a small Avenue of Honour commemorating those who served in World War I; head around the back to see the Aleppo pine that's a cutting taken from Gallipoli of the original Lone Pine.

● **NEXT UP** you'll cross busy Portarlington Rd at the traffic lights where the original old, rusty train tracks come into view. And while you may not have predicted golf to be on the cards for today's ride, hear us out: this next stop is a ripper. Marking the halfway point, **Curlewis Golf Club** (curlewisgolf.com.au) is the perfect pit stop for a burger and a beer (or just a coffee and a sandwich, if you're more sensible than us); but it's the driving range here that's all the rage. Attracting a young hip crowd, this is not golf as you know it, but rather a fun social day out with jugs of beer and a bucket of balls to whack out of the park. There's mini golf too, as well as the option of a sneaky little detour across the way to visit **Leura Park Estate** (leuraparkestate.com.au) for wine tasting – all the while remembering you've still got a long ride ahead of you! It's one of many stops along the region's **Bellarine Taste Trail** (thebellarinetastetrail.com.au) that takes in cool-climate wineries, gourmet food producers, a gin distillery and breweries.

⊙ **IT'S THEN BACK ON THE** bike to push on through to the historical township of **Drysdale**, where, across from its bird-filled lake, its oh-so-quaint heritage train station houses a museum inside the former stationmaster's residence. And while we mentioned earlier the train no longer passes through this way, that's not entirely true. Thanks to the **Bellarine Railway** (bellarinerailway.com.au), restored locomotives still chug back and forth from here to Queenscliff. And though the whole point of a rail trail is to ride your bike, if you did want to add some variety to your day, the heritage trains do take bicycles if you want to hitch a ride for the remaining 16km (or otherwise consider it for the return trip); check timetables before setting out.

⊙ **AFTER DRYSDALE,** the trail turns to compact gravel as you bump along past pastoral landscapes and olive groves, and from where the trail becomes bit of an undulating slog. You'll work up bit of a sweat (and possibly regret that burger and beer) but it's a particularly peaceful stretch, so try to take it all in. Scenic **Suma Park railway** is next, and though it's not an original station (instead built as a stop for the tourist railway); it's a lovely location nestled among vineyards with a well-tended garden along its platform.

⊙ **PEDAL ON** to cross Portarlington–Queenscliff Rd from where you'll get your first whiff of the briny coastal air as you're buoyed by the sign saying there's only 5.7km to go. Follow the backstreets along Old Port Rd to reach **Lonsdale Tomato Farm** (lonsdaletomatofarm.com), which feels like a bit of a secret find with a lovely rustic provedore selling local produce if you want to make up a gourmet picnic hamper.

⊙ **FROM HERE** you'll skirt the coastal township of Point Lonsdale before the trail loops around to briefly join quiet Murray Rd as the views open out to brackish Swan Bay. For those who don't like riding on the road, hang on tight, and rest assured that it's only a short leg along the road before you rejoin the designated bike path that runs parallel to the main road where pine trees form another World War I Avenue of Honour. The 'Welcome to Queenscliff' sign is a relief for that aching bike bum as you hit the home straight. Keep an eye out for info boards and hidden viewpoints offering insights to the bay's rich biodiversity, before pulling into **Queenscliff's** grand train station to complete your ride.

⚑ **HOPEFULLY YOU'RE IN NO GREAT RUSH TO RETURN,** as there's a bit to take in here – so lock up the bike to soak up the town's 19th-century maritime atmosphere as you stroll its quaint streetscape lined with heritage architecture. The **Queencliff Brewhouse** (queenscliffbrewhouse.com.au) is the perfect first stop for any weary, thirsty traveller and a fitting place to celebrate your arrival by sampling its beers and gins produced onsite. You can also pedal up to visit the historical Queenscliff Fort, the maritime museum and the harbour looking out to the Rip. Here you may see a ferry passing by, which is another option for you to continue your adventure across to the other side in Sorrento (searoad.com.au). But, to be honest, that's probably a stretch, so instead enjoy your afternoon before taking the leisurely ride (or train) back to Geelong – which itself has plenty of stuff to check out, including the sparkling **waterfront**, fantastic **gallery** (geelonggallery. org.au) and some cool city laneway bars and restaurants that'll defy any preconceptions that Geelong's some dreary backwater. By this stage you've probably missed the last ferry home (which leaves around 4pm), but don't worry: there are plenty of trains back through to Melbourne to bring you home by early evening.

Local Chit-chat with Jayne Tuttle

Jayne Tuttle, co-owner of The Bookshop at Queenscliff, theatre performer and acclaimed author of *Paris or Die* and *My Sweet Guillotine*.

What do you miss about the Bellarine Peninsula when you're overseas?

I miss the sea, the air, the starry sky at night. The sound of foghorns in winter, the ships bleating across the sea and into my bedroom. I miss the smell of the sweet salty air mixed with tea tree, the lazy moonahs, the cockatoos and rosellas and swans . . . nature and ships, that's what I miss most. The opposite of Paris.

Where do you take visitors to the Bellarine?

To swim, the crystal waters of Maytone beach at the end of Stevens St (shh, secret). To walk, the 'Lovers' Walk', a sandy track that runs behind the dunes between Queenscliff and Point Lonsdale (shh!). For wine and food, Noble Rot in Point Lonsdale has the relaxed feel and fine flavours of a Parisian corner bistrot; we are also die-hard fans of Sober Ramen in Geelong. For lunch and coffee, Queenscliff General Store, Bricktown, Piknik or Go Cafe in Geelong. For art, Queenscliff Gallery and Salt Gallery. For curiosity, Queenscliff Maritime Museum.

What do you think the bookshop means to the local community?

We took over the bookshop a few months before Covid. The value the community places on books and ideas and sharing has been staggering and inspiring. It's made it a real joy for us, even in the toughest times, and created a special closeness between us and the locals. The store has become a real cornerstone for people, a place to wander and think, flip through pages, chat.

CLICK, READ, LISTEN AND WATCH:

🌐 railtrails.org.au/trails/bellarine-rail-trail

📖 Kerry Greenwood, *Dead Man's Chest*
Bored, *Bored – This was Geelong*

BASS COAST RAIL TRAIL

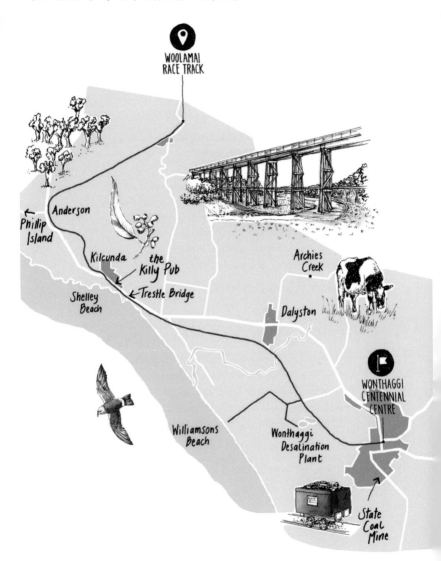

WOOLAMAI
RACE TRACK

Phillip
Island

Anderson

Kilcunda

the
Killy Pub

Shelley
Beach

Trestle Bridge

Archies
Creek

Dalyston

WONTHAGGI
CENTENNIAL
CENTRE

Williamsons
Beach

Wonthaggi
Desalination
Plant

State
Coal
Mine

START
Woolamai Race Track

FINISH
Wonthaggi Centennial Centre

DISTANCE
23.4km one-way

DURATION
3–6 hours return

TRANSPORT
Bikes aren't permitted on V-Lines buses, but if you're organised you can take the train to Stony Point for a ferry connection to Cowes on Phillip Island where buses (which will carry a bike) depart for Wonthaggi.

CONNECTING RIDES
East Gippsland Trail

George Bass Trail

Grandridge Rail Trail

Great Southern Rail Trail

Following the old Wonthaggi railway line is this scenic bike trail that mixes spectacular beaches, rolling dairy farms, gourmet produce and a fascinating local history. And with stops for pubs, ice-cream and bracing dips in the ocean, you'll be glad you dragged yourself off the couch to get out of the city for the day.

THERE'S SOMETHING SPECIAL about cycling a rail trail. For one, they feel a bit more hidden away than your ordinary bike path, and two, it feels like they're somehow keeping history alive: honouring the local stories, characters and events that would otherwise be lost to the past. And that's exactly what you'll do along the Bass Coast Rail Trail, a route that follows the old Wonthaggi line, where from 1910 till 1978 trains chugged by these scenic pastures through South Gippsland's historic coalmining areas.

🚴 **CYCLING WITH KIDS: Kilcunda** is the first stop, for burgers and milkshakes before spending some time by the beach. Detour to the **desalination plant**, then it's on to the wonderful **Williamsons Beach.** Visit the **State Coal Mine** in Wonthaggi before finishing up at the old train station, which houses a museum open on weekends. You can make a weekend out of this by tacking on a ride to Phillip Island for more family fun.

🟡 **THOUGH IT IS POSSIBLE TO GET HERE** by public transport and be back to Melbourne the same day, it's a mission that should only be taken by the super organised. It's one that involves a train, a ferry and a bus, all *before* you embark on your ride, and then doing the same to get back! Your mission, should you choose to accept it, will involve checking all the timetables with painstaking precision (for both directions) to ensure a smooth connection for what is a train to Stony Point to meet the ferry (westernportferries.com.au) over to Cowes in Phillip Island and then a local bus (southcoastbus.com.au) will deliver you and your bike to the trailhead at Wonthaggi to begin your ride.

If that all sounds utterly exhausting, just jump in the car and you'll be in **Woolamai** (the other end of trail) in around 90 minutes. Not to be confused with Cape Woolamai, which confusingly is nearby in Phillip Island, the Woolamai you're after is the rural inland municipality best known for its picturesque country **racetrack** (country.racing.com/woolamai). Each year from January to February it brings in the crowds for its annual picnic meets that have been run here since 1888.

🔵 **IT'S A RATHER UNCEREMONIOUS START**, with not as much as a sign to signify the beginning of the trail that leads off McGrath Rd. A dirt track passes the old Woolamai train station, which now is no more than an overgrown grassy platform, but back in the day it's where frocked-up fillies and suited gents would arrive by the trainload for a day at the races. And though there's talk of extending the trail to Nyora – where the original rail line originated – it's one step at a time, especially given the trail was only just recently extended from Anderson.

Although the start of the trail isn't signed, any doubts you're going the wrong way will be assuaged once you see a directional marker appearing every 1km. The undulating gravel track continues among gum trees and farmland that looks out over French Island in the distance – Victoria's largest island, where koalas outnumber locals 300 to one!

🔵 **AFTER RIDING 6KM** you'll arrive at the first stop, **ANDERSON** (population 28), which these days is no more than a bus stop, carpark and toilet block, all where the train station was once located. You'll reach a fork in the trail as the road splits at the roundabout to Phillip Island (where another dedicated bike–pedestrian trail leads to San Remo) and South Gippsland where the rail trail runs parallel to the Bass Hwy. (If you're taking the bus back to Cowes in Phillip Island, this is where your bike ride will finish). And just when you think there's not much to see here in Anderson, you'll pass **Artfusion Studio and Gallery** (`artfusionstudioandgallery.com`) a wonderful space to drop by to see sculpture and glasswork by two local artists.

As relaxed and picturesque as the ride has been so far, truth be told this first leg is all bit of a prelude for the next section when you'll get your first glimpse of South Gippsland's rugged coastal wilderness. This downhill stretch also takes in remnants from the region's coalmining days as you ride by the rusty remains of **Mitchell Mine** that produced 260,000 tons of black coal from 1908 to 1946. From here, the path crosses over the Bass Hwy to make its way into historic township of **Kilcunda** where the trail winds along the ocean, overlooking Bass Strait.

➤ **HERE IS THE START OF ANOTHER TRAIL,** the **George Bass Coastal Walk**, a spectacular 7km clifftop trail to San Remo, where British explorer George Bass embarked on his voyage back in 1798. And while ol' Georgie boy seems to have his name on everything out this way, of course long before his arrival the Bunurong People were here for millennia: evidence of charcoal and feasts of shellfish are scattered throughout these dunes. To see one of the area's nicest beaches you can take this trail down to **Shelley Beach** for a look around rockpools, and possibly a quick dip too; but at this point it's important to note this is a coastline not to be messed with; it's a treacherous stretch notorious for rips and sharks, so be sure not to venture in beyond your waist.

➤ **NEXT UP** you'll spot the iconic Killy Pub, a good reason to cross back over the highway again. One of coastal Gippsland's most famous pubs, the Tudor-style **Kilcunda Ocean View Hotel** (`kilcundaoceanviewhotel.com.au`) has been a favourite local watering hole for over 100 years, sought after for its coastal views, quality pub food and an all-Gippsland drinks list. Next door is the equally popular **Kilcunda General Store** (kilcunda-general-store.com), a perfect pit stop for ice-creams and milkshakes or otherwise delicious brekkies, burgers and beers from local microbreweries and wineries. It's a tough choice which one to choose, and to complicate things further there's another option in **Udder and Hoe** (udderandhoe.com.au), a charming provedore specialising in Gippsland gourmet produce and a wonderful place to stock up on local cheeses, wine, dips and breads to enjoy as a picnic hamper over the road at Kilcunda's pretty beach.

⊙ **ONCE YOU'RE DONE DECIDING** on which epicurean spot to indulge in, you'll arrive at another of Kilcunda's famous landmarks: its historic **trestle bridge**. Dating to 1911, this beautiful heritage-listed timber railway bridge stands 12m high and stretches 91m across Bourne Creek to offer sublime views across this rugged surf coast. And as you pedal on further by Kilcunda beach you'll start to wonder if this in fact is Australia's most scenic bike trail.

⊙ **AS YOU RIDE** by the cemetery, the trail heads inland over the Mouth of Powlett Rd for a 3km stretch through grasslands and dairy farms where kangaroos are regularly spotted before passing the next ghost station in **Dalyston**, where again there's little to no trace of the station. For those who are here to make a weekend of it, look no further than a 4.5km ride north to **Archies Creek Hotel** (archiescreekhotel.com.au) a winning combo where country pub meets rock'n'roll venue for a memorable night of live music and great food.

⊙ **BUT IF A DAY IS ALL YOU HAVE**, make your way over another trestle bridge to cross Powlett River where an off-trail detour awaits at Lower Powlett Rd for a short ride down to the **Wonthaggi Desalination Plant** (aquasure.com.au). Completed in 2013, this controversial project was constructed to address Melbourne's water catchment issues (which dropped to just above 25 per cent during the Millennium drought) by using reverse osmosis technology to desalinate sea water. While you can't go inside the plant, there's a signboard detailing the process. There's also an interesting ecological restoration project with extensive revegetation creating a coastal park with boardwalk and **bird hide**, where twitchers can tick off various species of waterbirds. Out here you'll also spot kangaroos, maybe an echidna and sometimes wombats and emus, too, as well snakes, so take care! But the other reason to come out here is **Williamsons Beach**, a sublime stretch of rugged coastline that'll appeal to those who like their beaches wild and remote.

◉ **PASSING** the giant spinning blades of the wind farm you'll arrive at the outskirts of Wonthaggi as the **State Coal Mine Historic Area** comes into view. Making up a part of the region's underground ring of black-coal mines, this is an industry (which operated from 1909 to 1968) that sprang up in response to a NSW coalmining strike that threatened Victoria's supplies. It was a set of circumstances that led to the development of the Wonthaggi State Coal Mine to tap into the region's vast deposits of black gold. In its time, the mine produced 16.74 million tons, making it Victoria's largest black-coal producer (and the fourth largest in Australia), powering the state's trains and industry.

Working in the coalmines was dangerous business, and many mining disasters occurred during the mine's history (including in 1937 when 13 men were killed) so a fitting first place to stop is the heritage-listed red-brick **Rescue Station**. Dating to 1928, it's one of the few remaining buildings; it stored rescue equipment and housed a smoke tunnel that was used to conduct underground rescue training. Today it serves as the **Rescue Station Arts** (rescuestationarts.org.au), offering all number of community activities and art exhibitions.

◉ **ACROSS THE WAY** you'll pass the Wonthaggi Pony Club, but back in the day the only ponies around this way were the pit ponies; much-loved, but hard-luck workhorses bred for the job of being down the mine and who lived in stables next to the rescue station. But if you think they had a tough life, spare a thought for the poor canaries who, likewise, resided next to the rescue station, and played a purely sacrificial role, being brought underground to detect toxic gases in the mines.

⊙ **TODAY**, Parks Victoria manages the area, and there are several walking trails leading you among the pits, shafts, sinkholes and old brickworks, as well a trail that leads over cinder from the old powerhouse boilers. There's also **Baxters Wetland Bird Hide** where along the way you'll find wild apple trees that have sprung up here from when miners tossed out their apple cores.

⊙ **AS YOU CONTINUE ALONG** the rail trail to reach the home straight, the appropriately historic **Wonthaggi Railway Station** awaits: a handsome Edwardian brick building (with a distinct Queen Anne–style twist) housing a **history museum** (`wonthaggihistoricalsociety.org.au`). Though the museum is only open on Saturdays, at other times you can check out the poppet head that blows its whistle at noon each day, as well a historic bullock dray parked on the old platform. And further ahead is the **Wonthaggi Centennial Centre** visitor centre, where you can collect a bunch of tourist brochures for onward travel, and have a look at its attached **ArtSpace gallery** (`artspacewonthaggi.com.au`) featuring exhibitions by local artists.

And if you think you're done here, think again. Not only has a new trail extension just been announced to link Wonthaggi to **Inverloch** via an inland farmland route (estimated to be completed any time in 2023–25) but there's also the town itself to explore. In keeping with the theme of this rail trail, the **State Coal Mine** (`parkstay.vic.gov.au/state-coal-mine`) is Wonthaggi's main must-see sight, not only for underground mine tours (sadly not available until further notice due to maintenance), but a for a deep dive into the area's mining history.

⚑ **FROM HERE** it's either back on the bike for the return ride, or jump on a bus back to either Anderson station to ride back to Woolamai, or stay on till the end of the line to Cowes – where obviously there's plenty to do on Phillip Island. Otherwise jump back on the ferry to get back on the train back to Melbourne. No doubt you'll sleep very well!

Local Chit-chat with Lou Storti

Lou Storti emigrated from the mountains of Italy to join his father working underground in the coalmines in Wonthaggi. It was a big shock, but he soon got used to it, making friends and eventually falling love. These days you'll still find him underground, volunteering as a tour guide.

You immigrated to Australia from Italy in 1949; has the area changed much over the years?

It has changed a lot. In 1950 there were horse and jinkers; now there are so many cars, it is hard to find somewhere to park. In those days, you knew your neighbours, which is not so much the case these days. Old people used to teach young people skills, and now that role has reversed; however, I feel the young people don't have the time to teach the older people the skills. When the State Coal Mine ceased operations in 1968, many of the men moved away from Wonthaggi to find jobs in other factories or mines. It was thought Wonthaggi would become a bit of a ghost town. It managed to survive all these years and is now bustling, with a lot of people moving from Melbourne to settle in the country.

The old train line is now a bicycle trail, so what were your memories of the train itself?

I remember the train very well, and used to take it to Melbourne some weekends, and to Kilcunda over the Christmas holidays to meet up with some of my family and go swimming at the beach. The train ride was always very scenic going through Kilcunda, as you could see the ocean.

What was your job in the mines?

I started out at the mines as a clipper at the age of 19. A clipper helped in clipping the skips of coal onto the rope, which winched the skips out the mine. I then became a wigger and was given a horse to teach commands to, so that it could pull skips in the underground mine.

At the age of 21, I became a miner, which I enjoyed because it paid relatively well, and you got more money if you worked harder. Something I did not enjoy was if there was water on the mine floor and I'd have to lie in it to dig for coal. But everyone got used to it, as it was all part of being a miner.

You have been a volunteer tour guide at the State Coal Mine for some years now?

I have met a lot of great people over the years as a guide at the State Coal Mine. One story I like to tell visitors is that in 1968 when the mines were closed, me and my brothers took over the mine privately and tried to continue mining coal. However, we stopped the venture as we did not make any money. Me and my brother decided to try growing mushrooms underground, which we did, however no one wanted those either!

CLICK, READ, LISTEN AND WATCH:

railtrails.org.au/trails/bass-coast-rail-trail
wonthaggihistoricalsociety.org.au

Joe Chambers and Lyn Chambers, *Come Here! Gee Off! Wonthaggi's State Coal Mine Pit Ponies*
Mark Cauchi, Rails by the Sea: *The Remarkable Story of Kilcunda's Railway History*

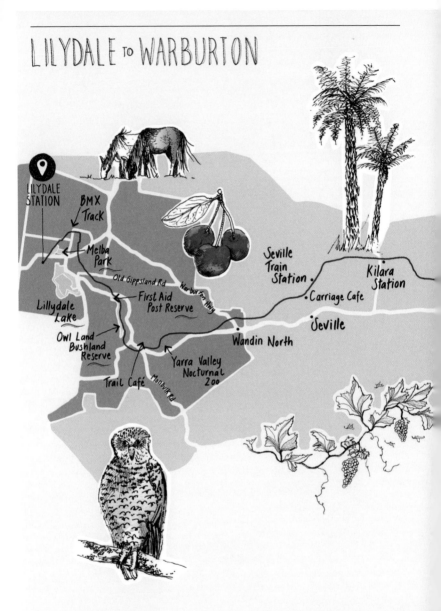

LILYDALE TO WARBURTON

LILYDALE STATION

BMX Track

Melba Park

Old Gippsland Rd

First Aid Post Reserve

Warburton Hwy

Lillydale Lake

Owl Land Bushland Reserve

Trail Café

Monbulk Rd

Yarra Valley Nocturnal Zoo

Wandin North

Seville Train Station

Carriage Cafe

Seville

Kilara Station

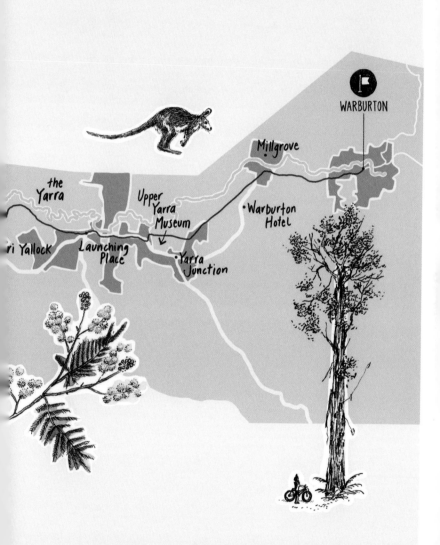

the
Yarra

Upper
Yarra
Museum

ri Yallock

Launching
Place

Yarra
Junction

Millgrove

Warburton
Hotel

WARBURTON

START
Lilydale

FINISH
Warburton

DISTANCE
40km (one-way)

DURATION
6-8 hours return

Lilydale train station marks the beginning of the trail. If driving, you can park at the station or down a side street, but check parking signs carefully. If you're not up for the return ride you can jump on a bus (martyrs.com.au) but there are only two spots for bikes.

CONNECTING RIDES
Bay Trail (p40)

Carrum to Warburton Trail

Olinda Creek Trail

O'Shannassy Aqueduct Trail

Yarra Valley Trail

Riding alongside the rails of the ol' train line from Lilydale to Warburton is this rousing journey through the eclectic nature-filled landscapes of the Yarra Ranges. It's a trail passing mature tree fern gullies and manna gum forest in between farm landscapes and a string of historical communities filled with charming cafes, pubs and museums.

THERE'S ALWAYS ONE must-ride-trail on every list, and far as we're concerned this it: the Warby Trail. The perfect ride to get out of town and reset in revitalising fresh country air. We say 'get out of town', but somehow this forested rail trail that runs through the Yarra Ranges still constitutes metropolitan Melbourne, a boundary that seems especially confounding once you hit the farmland region – something not lost on locals either, after being roped into Melbourne's contentious Covid lockdowns.

🚲 **CYCLING WITH KIDS:** Detour to **Lillydale Lake** for the playground and small beach. Maybe meet a horse at **Trail Cafe**. The **Yarra Valley Nocturnal Zoo** will be very popular. **Tommy Finn's Trout Farm** (`facebook.com/tommyfinnstroutfarm`) is a fun way to break up the ride. Along the trail, look out for whimsical features from dressed-up wooden spoons to monkeys hiding in trees. Beyond Warburton, there's **Warburton Water World** (`facebook.com/WarburtonWaterWorld`), perfect for cooling off in summer. If you're staying overnight, you can ride to the **Rainforest Gallery** to walk among the treetops, or the very Instagrammable **Californian Redwood Forest**.

◉ **WHILE THIS IS A RURAL RIDE**, the getting-here bit is a breeze. Whether driving or jumping on the Lilydale line, you'll be here in just under an hour. And though Lilydale is known as the end of the line, here locals instead prefer to say it's just the beginning; as it's the gateway to both the Yarra Valley and Dandenong Ranges, who are we to disagree?

Lilydale may be unmistakeably the outer suburbs, but among the brash signage of takeaway and retail outlets, you'll still catch glimpses of country life. It has a more relaxed feel with fresher air, heritage tree–lined streets, historic pubs and 19th-century buildings, including the Victorian-era **Yarra Ranges Regional Museum** (`yarraranges.vic.gov.au/experience/yarra-ranges-regional-museum`), in a former bank, and the **Lilydale Athenaeum Theatre** (`lilydaleatc.com`). Both are located in **Melba Park**, which is named after Lilydale's most famous resident, Dame Nellie Melba (1861–1931), the world-renowned opera singer who's buried in Lilydale Cemetery.

◉ **BUT BACK AT THE STATION**, on the main road you can get a good locally roasted coffee at **Locavore Cafe** (`locavorestudio.com.au`) before dropping by **Yarra Valley Cycles** (`yarravalleycycles.com`) for all your bike trail needs. As well as having maps, advice and toilet amenities, they sell bike accessories and puncture repair kits, which is something you'll definitely need for this journey. More importantly, here you can also hire a bike through **Ridetime Yarra Valley** (`ridetimeyarravalley.com.au`) who rent out a range of electric bikes, a very popular choice for the undulating path ahead.

◉ **AT THIS POINT** we should also mention that if you don't want to drive or catch the train, it's feasible to cycle here from Melbourne. You'll need to be fit, though, as it's a route that's going to add to what could already be a 100-km ride. So while it's anything but a shortcut, if you're game and have time on your side, it's a great ride that links Melbourne's dedicated bike paths: Sandridge Rail Trail–Bay Trail–Dandenong Creek Trail–Taralla Creek Trail–Olinda Creek Trail–Lilydale. Exhausting, yes, but if you're looking for an epic 'local' ride, it's a good excuse to make a weekend of it.

FOR THE OTHER 99.99 PER CENT OF RIDERS OUT THERE, if you just want to get going from Lilydale station, cross to the other side of Maroondah Hwy to pass the original heritage-listed train station where the bike trail leads on through to Lilydale Reserve. This is home to the Lilydale Football Club, a team established back in 1872, making it not only one of Australia's oldest football teams, but one of the oldest of any code in the world. Here signs for the rail trail direct you to the official beginning of the ride at Beresford Rd, where between 1901 and 1965 the historical train line ran between Lilydale and Warburton to transport both passengers and goods.

It's also the starting point for the region's newest ride, the **Yarra Valley Trail**. Unveiled in 2022, this 12km bike path runs to Yarra Glen via Yering; it's part of a masterplan to link up the trail with Healesville. But that's one for another time, as today our focus lies on the Warby trail.

STARTING OFF with a slight ascent, the trail takes you by a very cool BMX track; its gnarly jumps and embankments may tempt you to trade in the mountain bike for a BMX to hang out here instead! But before you know it, you're coasting down Nelson Rd, where the trail makes a sharp right to run alongside the high school. Here you'll suck in a few deep breaths to prepare for a steep 125m climb, a section that back in the day even steam trains needed added fuel to tackle. And as you chug up in second gear, regretting not getting that e-bike, just remember that at least you're exercising – unlike those e-cheats who power up without even breaking into a sweat!

◐ **ONCE YOU'VE REACHED THE TOP**, stick to the left to ride over the rusty steel bridge that leads over the six-lane Maroondah Hwy. Ahead lies an optional scenic detour to **Lillydale Lake** (500m one-way), which, along with a yacht club, has possibly what is Melbourne's only inland beach (but it's one more for the kids), along with remnants of a historic 1850s flour mill.

◐ **TRUCKIN' ON**, you'll cross over the Old Gippsland Rd, where you'll need to take care for traffic that comes flying down the hill. It's one of many road crossings you'll encounter during the ride, so be sure to always come to a complete stop to look both ways for cars that come through faster than you think. Across the road you can fill up your water bottle as you stop to take in views of Mt Dandenong looming in the distance.

◐ **AT THIS POINT** the trail has passed mainly through outlying residential zones, but once you cross into Mt Evelyn things become noticeably bushier. Riding along the cool shady path of a pine forest, you'll shoot through a barrel-shaped tunnel to reach the **First Aid Post Reserve.** This land was originally owned by David Mitchell (famous for building Melbourne's Exhibition Building, as well as being the father of Dame Nellie Melba) until it was donated by the family for the railways to conduct their First Aid Competitions. Held from 1911 to 1992, these mock competitions comprised teams of railway centres from around Australia treating 'patients' in a range of hypothetical situations. While this hardly sounds like a spectator sport, the fact that there was a drinking tent on hand suggests otherwise.

◐ **NEXT ALONG** you'll ride by the **Owl Land Bushland Reserve** (yarraranges.vic.gov.au/Experience/Parks-Recreation/Owlands-Reserve) a conservation area for the powerful owl – one of only two dedicated owl reserves in the world. It's a name these carnivorous predators live up to, feeding on a diet mainly of possums that they lift up with their strong talons to feast upon in the trees; anyone familiar with the thunderous racket of brush-tails living in their roof will know these things aren't small! Here a nature trail leads through the old-growth forest, and, though you'd be lucky to see an owl, you can sometimes see their pellet droppings that contain remnants of possum bones at the base of trees, so you can tell where their nests are. For more information visit the website of MEEPA (Mt Evelyn Environment Protection and Progress Association; meeppa.org.au).

So far there's been no real suggestion this trail was once a former railway line, and given the tracks were removed in the 1970s, that's not surprising. As you ride on, that changes when you pull up to the platform at the old Mt Evelyn station. If you're feeling a little puffed at this point, that's because this right here is the highest point of the line (225m), so it's a good time to take a breather and a look around. As well as the old stationmaster's house (which has been converted into Mt Evelyn Community House), the train platform is lined with decorative bollards and info on local titbits, including the time when Queen Elizabeth and Prince Philip passed through here on the train to give the royal wave back in 1954. There's also an acknowledgement to the Wurundjeri People, who've resided in this area for many thousands of years before European settlement, spending their time between wetlands and woodlands around Mt Evelyn.

This is also a handy spot for a toilet break and maybe a coffee at **Billy Goat Hill Brasserie** (billygoathill.net.au), a modern cafe along Mt Evelyn's main strip that back in the day was a popular holiday destination for Melburnians. The suburb even added the 'Mount' prefix to its name back in 1919 as a marketing ploy to lure them in!

⊜ **CONTINUING ALONG** you'll cross over busy York Rd to enjoy a racy downhill section through Mt Evelyn's forested interior. At Monbulk Rd you'll cross again at the lights to reach the tin shed **Trail Cafe** (thetrailcafe.com), a popular stop for cyclists with a menu of toasties, homemade sausage rolls and milkshakes. Its wood-fire heater adds to its country charm, and so does the fact that it's horse friendly. Yes, that's right: you can bring along your own horse in what is most likely the only place in Melbourne in 100 years with a dedicated spot to tie up your saddlehorse.

◉ **AHEAD** is another stop to consider, a short five-minute detour down Littlejohn Ave to **Yarra Valley Nocturnal Zoo** (`yarravalleynocturnalzoo.com.au`). Set up by a local couple, this private zoo is a showcase of Australian native wildlife and where visitors can pat a dingo and a koala, along with hundreds of animals including crocs, snakes and the rare southern brush-tailed rock wallaby, a species with only 60 or so remaining in the wild. The zoo also does wonderful work in supporting people in the community with disabilities.

◉ **BACK ON THE TRAIL**, after that climb to Mt Evelyn, you'll enjoy a further luxurious downhill section as you fly by gullies of tree ferns and gum trees before the scenery opens up to the farmland surrounds of Wandin North. This here is fruit-growing country, and you'll still find orchards that date back to the 1870s growing berries, apples and cherries. And you know you've officially hit rural pastures when suddenly you find yourself having to dodge horse manure on the path!

◉ **AFTER A FEW MORE** bridge and road crossings you'll ride over the Warburton Hwy to reach Wandin and its old train station platform that's painted in local-themed **murals** (`facebook.com/wandinhistoricmuralproject`). And if you missed the native wildlife at the stop before, look up and you might find a local variety: bright, furry and slightly terrifying soft-toy monkeys that people have put up in the trees to bring a bit of colour to the trail.

◉ **PUSHING ON ALONG** the bushy trail you'll next arrive at Seville, where it now feels more appropriate to call these places 'towns' rather than 'suburbs'. Here's another fairly unexpected sight as the **Carriage Café** (`carriagecafe.com.au`) manifests itself from the bush. It's a historic 110-year-old train carriage converted to a cafe doing a seasonal menu of locally driven produce that makes the perfect stop for lunch or coffee. The carriage itself isn't actually from this train route, but rather from the Albury to Seymour line.

➡ RAMPING UP THE RANDOM STAKES, next is Seville station with its quirky wooden spoon collection that sits along the station platform. Here the locals have dressed spoons up as everything from Santa to the Fab Four.

As you try to figure out what that's all about, you'll pedal on to reach idyllic landscapes of the Yarra Ranges that unveil themselves like you've just ridden into the canvas of an Australian Impressionist masterpiece. The added bonus of vineyards brings another layer of beauty to the scene. So by the time you reach Kilara station, you're now well and truly in the country, regardless of what any arbitrary LGA boundary may tell you.

➡ IT'S THEN ANOTHER UPHILL RIDE before hitting a dead straight section for another 4km to cross over bridges and past grazing cows to reach Woori Yallock, a name from the local Wurundjeri dialect that means 'running creek'. Pulling in to the train station's platform you're probably starting to feel a bit of saddle soreness at this point, so it's a good spot to park the bike and fill up your water bottle for bit of a break. Along the platform are more photographs and murals celebrating the district, including a rare shot of the steam train charging through here.

➡ CONTINUE ALONG these provincial scenes for another 6km to arrive at the township of Launching Place. It's here you'll run into an old familiar face in the Yarra River, though it's sneakily hidden, and with no sign you could easily be forgiven for not knowing it was even there. But it was from the edge of these waters that the town got its name, when freshly cut timber logs were 'launched' down the river to float along to Melbourne's sawmills. It's also here where boats were launched to bring the supplies to nearby gold diggings. But it's the pub across the road that's Launching Place's most prominent landmark; a double-storey terrace hotel (est. 1902) that resembles a gunslinger saloon from the Wild West. It was closed for renovations at the time we visited, but it should be open by the time you ride by.

⊙ **FROM HERE** the trail crosses over the Warburton Hwy to reach another rest stop to fill up your water bottle, before reaching Launching Place's train station that's in name only, with no platform. The trail then curves down alongside the highway before crossing over to the next township at Yarra Junction. As if to make up for the previous station's lack of showing, Yarra Junction actually has a train station, the only surviving one on the trail. And it's a beauty too. Built in 1888, this building was actually Lilydale's original train station before being relocated here to Yarra Junction in 1915. Today it forms part of the **Upper Yarra Museum** (uyvhs.org.au) that covers both the railway and local history; it's only open Sundays, so, unless you can make it then, you may have to settle for seeing the old railway guard carriage and tramway rail tractor from the outside. But otherwise a further reason to come on a Sunday is for Yarra Junction's market that takes place on the second and fourth Sundays of each month from 8am to 2pm.

Also along the trail is a series of sculptures by prolific artist Glenn Romanis. These include the *Junction*, timber tram tracks that represent what was Victoria's largest logging area, and a piece designed to decay over time, and contrasted with *Always been here, always will be*, a mosaic depicting the permanence of these ancient lands, which was built using fossilised seed ferns and petrified wood.

The trail passes through an Avenue of Honour commemorating Anzacs who served in World War I, before passing a trail-side cafe from where you can venture on to the main shopping strip to the local bike shop **Girt by Dirt** (girtxdirt.com) for cycling tours, rental, maintenance, and if you haven't got one yet, a spare puncture kit for the rocky road ahead.

◉ **LEAVING YARRA JUNCTION**, the trail deviates north-east from the highway to lead through more wonderful natural scenery. There's always one point in a ride where you'll start to feel a little bit over things as fatigue kicks in, and that point could just about be now, but with under 10km remaining, hang in there: you're on the home straight. While the trail skirts the town of Wesburn, it's a tempting option to take a short ride to visit the region's oldest – dating to 1863 – pub, the heritage-listed **Warburton Hotel** (warburtonhotel.com. au), which is a good spot to sample Yarra Valley's famed local wines and beers. But otherwise, you'll ride by Wesburn's train station (or the sign anyway) before reaching the pleasant little town of Millgrove. Here you'll pass the town's shops before continuing along its Avenue of Honour to the old train station sign. If you're here on the third Saturday or fifth Sunday of the month you can check out Millgrove Market to pick up some local wares, including a bottle from **Yarra Valley Whisky** (yarravalleywhisky.com.au), a local distiller doing bottles of gin, rum and moonshine.

◉ **YOU'LL THEN HIT** the paved section of the trail for the final 3.3km stretch into Warburton, where you'll arrive to the agreeable sight of what is a charming historical town that makes for a fitting end to this long ride. The 19th-century **Alpine Hotel** (alpineretreat.com.au) is the first place you'll pass with an enticing beer garden that beckons for a post-ride celebratory drink. Recently renovated to retain its old world charm, the Alpine is one of Warburton's best places for cyclists to stay, with both an atmospheric front bar and bistro, and well-priced accommodation. Next along is **Cog Bike Cafe** (cogbikesaustralia. com.au) another Warby favourite that looks out for battle-weary riders in need of a cold drink and a feed, as well as operating as a bike shop and **bike hire** (warburtonbikehire.com.au) for both onward rides, or to begin your ride in Lilydale. Then just a bit further along you'll come across that magical sight of the Warburton train station sign to mark the official ending of the trail.

⊘ **FROM THIS POINT** many cyclists simply just jump back on the bike to do the return ride to Lilydale, but if you're not up for a return 40km ride (which you'll need a pretty good fitness base to do), there's the option to put your bike on Bus 683 that heads back to Lilydale station. The only hitch here is that there are only two bike racks (and you can't book ahead), so if you're in a group you may have to work it out using rock, paper, scissors. Weekends and busy times can also be bit of a punt, but if you want to maximise your chances of securing the coveted bike rack, there's always the sneaky option to ride to the next bus stop ahead (but you didn't hear that from us).

⊘ **THE BEST OPTION** in our opinion is to hang around; if not for the night, at least for a few hours to soak up Warburton's atmospheric main strip that tempts with options of ice-cream (`warburtonicecream.com.au`), pizza (`facebook.com/warburtonlittlejoe`), bakeries (`facebook.com/TheWarburtonBakery`) and coffee (`silvacoffee.com.au/pages/roastery-door`). There's also the Art Deco Arts Centre (c. 1934) and visitor centre at the waterwheel (that was used to power a nearby goldmine) for any brochures and tips on onward travel. For a meal with a view, don't miss **Riverview Cafe & Wine Bar** (`theriverview.com.au`) with its scenic vine-draped deck overlooking the Yarra River, which makes a special guest appearance as it courses its way through the back of town. To get a better look at this scenic bend of the Yarra, you can make your way to the **Warburton Swing Bridge** that dates to 1952. And if you're around on the second Saturday of each month there's a **market** (9am to 2pm), too.

⚑ FOR THOSE WHO CHOOSE TO HANG AROUND FOR A WEEKEND, there are plenty of options for outdoor bike adventures. Most popular is the **O'Shannassy Aqueduct Trail** that leads for 30km through the forests of mountain ash, manna gum and fern gullies of the Yarra Ranges National Park, home to wallabies, wombats, koalas, lyrebirds and kookaburras along a route that delivered water to the Melbourne area from 1914 till 1996. It's a trail that also links up to reach Californian redwood trees at Cement Creek Road, where you'll be immersed among these giants of the forest that soar 55m above. But whatever you decide – daytrip, weekend or beyond – the Yarra Ranges is an area made for two wheels, so be sure to make the most of it.

CLICK, READ, LISTEN AND WATCH:

🌐 lilydalehistorical.com.au
   warburtoninfo.com
   rideyarraranges.com.au
   yarraranges.vic.gov.au

📖 *Balit Bagurrk: Strong Aboriginal* and *Torres Strait Islander Women of the Yarra Ranges*

🎵 Augie March, 'The Cold Acre'

BUT WAIT, THERE'S MORE . . .

Additional rides through Melbourne's varied landscapes

In addition to the main trails covered in this book, there are plenty of other dedicated bike paths throughout the city to keep you busy pedalling across Melbourne. Some are scenic, some are suburban and some are downright gritty, but they all offer a chance to see another side of Melbourne and the chance to jump back on the bike for some adventure, exploration and exercise. Many bike paths are interconnected, allowing you to tailor your ride depending on your mood; you can make these anything from one-hour rides to several days. Here is a selection of trails worth getting back in the saddle for.

Federation Trail

 START
Fogarty Ave, Yarraville

 FINISH
Werribee River Park

 DISTANCE
24km one-way

 DURATION
4-6 hours return

 Spotswood, Aircraft, Werribee train stations

Covering Melbourne's industrial west is this bicycle ride out to Werribee alongside the path of the 19th-century Main Outfall Sewer pipeline. Sounds lovely, right? If you're worried it's going stink, rest assured: the sewer line linking Werribee to the old Spotswood Pumping Station was decommissioned back in the 1990s. The trail passes over creeks, bridges and all sorts of industry as you ride through Brooklyn, Laverton North and Hoppers Crossing, where you'll ride parallel to the Princess Hwy. Awaiting you in Werribee are a number of rewards including the **Werribee Open Range Zoo** (zoo.org.au/werribee), the **Werribee Park Precinct** (parks.vic.gov.au/places-to-see/parks/werribee-park) including its historic mansion and **Shadowfax Winery** (shadowfax.com.au). From here you take the train back, or otherwise if you want to cycle home via a different route you can join up with the Skeleton Creek Trail to ride along the **Hobsons Bay Coastal Trail** (p52).

Diamond Creek Trail

START
Wilson Rd, Wattle Glen

FINISH
Yarra River Trail, Eltham

DISTANCE
14km one-way

DURATION
2-3 hours return

Wattle Glen, Eltham train stations

A wonderful family ride for those seeking something with a more rural flavour is this trail through Melbourne's outer north-east suburbs. After the train trip to Wattle Glen, you'll ride up to the trailhead at Wattle Glen War Memorial Park to begin the journey running alongside Diamond Creek, where platypus are sometimes spotted, on the eucalyptus-lined path. Riding through Nillumbik Park, you'll pass Coventry Oval, which was named after Diamond Creek's favourite sons: Gordon and Syd Coventry, brothers and legendary Collingwood footballers from the 1920s glory days. Nearby **Golden Hills Brewery** (goldenhillsbrewery.com) makes a tempting stop, or continue down Diamond Creek Reserve to pass **Diamond Creek Rotary Tram Cafe** (facebook.com/DiamondCreekRotaryTramCafe) set in an old W-class tram. Crossing Allendale Rd, you'll move into Eltham and find the **Edendale Community Environment Farm** (edendale.vic.gov.au/Home), a 19th-century farm and heritage homestead that today is all about sustainability and community, with farm animals the kids can feed. Keep on winding down the trail through Eltham and the Barak Bushlands Reserve past the miniature railway at **Diamond Valley Railway Inc.** (dvr.com.au). Nearby is the Eltham Copper Butterfly Playspace, named after this local endangered species and featuring fully accessible equipment. From here the bike trail meets up with the bushy section of the Yarra River, where a bridge crosses over to link up with the Main Yarra Trail if you want to take the long ride back to Melbourne.

Djerring Trail

START
Caulfield station

FINISH
Dandenong station

DISTANCE
19km one-way

DURATION
3–5 hours return

Caulfield, Dandenong train stations

Running alongside the Pakenham and Cranbourne train lines, this suburban rail trail leads through Melbourne's south-east. This is another route that's not going to win any awards for the city's most scenic ride, but again, it's not always about looks, but rather getting you out and exploring areas you may not be familiar with. Starting out from Caulfield station (where you can join up with our St Kilda neighbourhood ride p40) you'll ride beneath the rail overpass to cruise through the suburbs of Carnegie, Murrumbeena, Hughesdale, Oakleigh, Clayton, Springvale and Noble Park, each with its own local character and flavours. And food is definitely a highlight along this ride, with multicultural delights in Springvale and Dandenong. Finishing up at the Dandenong station, you can from here link up with the EastLink Trail, jump on a train or ride back.

Dandenong Creek Trail

START
Carrum

FINISH
Liverpool Rd, Kilsyth South

DISTANCE
50km one-way

DURATION
8-10 hours return

Carrum, Dandenong, Bayswater train stations

This cross-city adventure offers a wonderful mix of scenery on a ride linking Melbourne's bayside to its far rural reaches. Starting off at Carrum, you'll cycle alongside the Patterson River from where the Dandenong Creek empties into Port Phillip Bay/Nerm. This is where you can join up with the **Bay Trail** (p40) into the city or to Mornington Peninsula, but the Dandenong Creek Trail takes the inland route as you ride by the boat launch area to follow the creek through Dandenong's reserves. Ahead, those with kids can make a stop at **Myuna Farm** (casey.vic.gov.au/facilities-hire/myuna-farm) to meet all the farm animals before moving on to Doveton, the Dandenong Wetlands and Tirhatuan Wetlands before crossing paths with the Peninsula Link Trail. Ride on through Rowville, Mulgrave and Wheelers Hill to stop in at **Chesterfield Farm** (chesterfieldfarm.com.au) or Jells Park, where, if you're around in 2061, you'll be able to spot Halley's Comet! Wantirna South, Glen Waverley and Vermont are the suburbs next up, offering everything from bird hides to pony clubs, before you'll ride through Heathmont to land at Marie Wallace Bayswater Park. Here you can take the ride to Puffing Billy (p102) or the Taralla Creek Trail to meet up with the Warby Trail (p192). Otherwise continue on through Bayswater before the trail finishes up at Kilsyth South, where you'll wave goodbye to the creek as it continues back to its origin in the foothills of the Dandenong Ranges.

M80/Western Ring Road Trail

 START
Merino St, Laverton North

 FINISH
Civic Dr, Greensborough

 DISTANCE
41km one-way

 DURATION
6–8 hours return

 Ardeer, Ginifer, Jacana, Diamond Creek train stations

This dedicated bike path is a swoop through Melbourne's north that runs parallel to the Western Ring Road. Cycling beside a highway may not sound like the world's most beautiful ride, and, truth be told, it's really not. But that's okay: not everything has to be picture perfect. Instead this is a rather industrialised trail, which in itself you could argue is its selling point, allowing you to check out some areas of Melbourne you may not know too well, and offering an excuse to head outdoors and get some exercise. It's a route that'll take you through the outskirts of suburbs such as Laverton North, Ardeer, Tullamarine, Gowanbrae, Glenroy, Thomastown, Bundoora and Greensborough – as well as other suburbs not covered in the guidebooks. Along the way you'll intersect with many other rides, allowing you to dip in and out of the Federation Trail, Maribyrnong River Trail and Moonee Creek Trail for the western suburbs; or Merri Creek, Northern Pipeline, Darebin Creek or Diamond Creek trails that lead down to various points along the Yarra River.

EastLink Trail

START
Springvale Rd, Donvale

FINISH
Dandenong bypass

DISTANCE
35km one-way

DURATION
6–8 hours return

Heatherdale, Yarraman train stations

It may run alongside the EastLink tollway, but you won't need an e-TAG for this ride as you make your way through Melbourne's outer eastern suburbs. Starting from Donvale, this ride connects with the creek trails of Koonung and Mullum Mullum creeks, but stick beside the freeway to pass **Schwerkolt Cottage Reserve** (whitehorsehistory.org.au) and its 19th-century cottage in Mitcham. Further on you'll cycle by reserves and parklands to cross into Ringwood and Vermont as you ride by Dandenong Creek, where you'll hit the creek trail and pass the **Australian Jazz Museum** (ajm.org.au) in Wantirna; a must for all hepcats out there. Along the way, keep an eye out for the public sculpture that dots the trail as part of the Artlink initiative. Ride across Blind Creek with another bike trail offshoot, and on to Scoresby to visit the old homestead at **Chesterfield Farm** (chesterfieldfarm.com.au). The ride then links up with the Dandenong Creek Trail, and you'll ride through Mulgrave and the Tirhatuan Wetlands to reach Dandenong North. Here at Yarraman station you can connect with the Djerring Trail, but stick to the trail where you'll cross the other side to ride beside Mile Creek to finish at Dandenong bypass. From here you can continue along the Dandenong Creek Trail that continues on through to the bayside suburb of Carrum.

Moonee Ponds Creek Trail

 START
Ron Barrasi Sr Park, Docklands

 DISTANCE
25km one-way

 FINISH
Marker Rd, Westmeadows

 DURATION
4–6 hours return

 Southern Cross, Macaulay, Flemington Bridge, Jacana, Pascoe Vale train stations

Snaking alongside an urban creek, this is a peaceful glide through Melbourne's inner north-west. Starting from the spot where Moonee Ponds Creek empties into Port Phillip Bay/Nerm, the trail takes you through the Docklands to join forces with the **Capital City Trail** (p28). And while at times this creek may feel more like a stormwater drain, recent conservation efforts have seen it cleaned up to bring birdlife and fish back to these waters. Following the creek, the trail runs by the train lines of gritty North Melbourne beneath the shadow of the CityLink overpass before you part ways with the Capital City Trail at Flemington Bridge to proceed northbound. Back on the suburban streets before riding by parkland, you'll pass by an impressive trestle bridge as you cycle through the suburbs of Travancore, Essendon, Moonee Ponds and Brunswick West. At Pascoe Vale you'll cut through 5 Mile Creek Reserve before winding again under the highway to ride through the green belts of Oak Park and Gowanbrae. Push on to Glenroy and Gladstone Park where the path intersects with the Western Ring Road Trail and continues on to a final long stretch through to Westmeadows, from where the creek continues on to its upper section in Greenvale.

Darebin Creek Trail

START
Willsmere Park, Kew East

FINISH
Cottage Blvd, Epping

DISTANCE
27.5km one-way

DURATION
5–6 hours return

 Epping, Darebin train stations

Another northbound option is this scenic ride that courses alongside Darebin Creek (friendsofdarebincreek.org.au) from Epping to the Yarra River. It starts off fast as you cycle through Porsche Park and Maserati Park (alongside Jaguar Ct and Lotus Ct), before continuing through parkland, reserves, wetlands and a series of interconnecting bike paths. Pass through Bundoora and Reservoir before reaching Heidelberg to ride by Northland shopping centre and on to Preston to stop off at **Moon Dog World** (moondogbrewing.com.au/world), a must-see set-up for beer lovers, with 72 taps on offer, along with its sparkling pool and waterfall centrepiece. Ride on through Thornbury and Alphington to arrive at the Yarra River, where the creek flows through beautiful natural parkland and billabongs. From here you'll meet up with the Main Yarra Trail where you can make your way into the city.

Northern Pipe Trail

START
Rushall station, North Fitzroy

DISTANCE
13 km one-way

FINISH
Thomastown station

DURATION
2-3 hours return

Rushall, Thomastown, Epping train stations

Following the underground pipe that brings in Melbourne's water supplies, this shared bike–pedestrian trail runs through the guts of Melbourne's inner north. You may already have cycled the St Georges Rd Trail bit on the **Northside** ride (p158) but this bike path stretches beyond Thornbury and Preston on through to Reservoir to finish at Thomastown train station. At the endpoint you'll meet up with the Western Ring Road Trail to lead you east–west, or you can take a shared bike path extending further 4.5km north along Dalton Rd to Epping station. The southern section starts out from Northcote, from where it joins up with the **Merri Creek Trail** (p84), before running through the median strip alongside the tram tracks.

Gardiners Creek

START
Yarra Blvd, Burnley

FINISH
Laburnum station, Blackburn

DISTANCE
17km one-way

DURATION
3-4 hours return

Kooyong, East Malvern, Alamein, Laburnum train stations

Highways and creeks are a theme for many of Melbourne's trails, and this ride's got 'em both. Meandering along Gardiners Creek, the path runs beside the Monash Fwy as you set out from St Kevin's College Boatshed to cross over the Yarra River at the cyclist bridge. Ride by the Kooyong Tennis Centre, the home of the Kooyong Classic – and the Australian Open before that where McEnroe and Navratilova graced the arena, and everyone from Led Zeppelin to the Rolling Stones played. Cycle again over the Yarra to zip through Hawthorn, where on Saturday you'll find the Boroondara Farmers Market (8am to 1pm), and then the Glen Iris Wetlands to take a look at its bird hide. Continue alongside this urban creek through Ashburton, where you can take note of Scotchmans Creek Trail for another day, before briefly linking up with the Anniversary Trail till you take a right through Markham Reserve through Malvern East and Ashwood. Crossing High St, the trail continues north into Burwood over the highway and into the outskirts of Box Hill South around the golf club. Over Canterbury Rd you'll land in Box Hill proper before the ride finishes up in Blackburn, where you'll make your way just north of Garie Street Playground to arrive at Laburnum station to take the train home.

Mullum Mullum Creek Trail

START
Main Yarra Trail, Templestowe

FINISH
Highland Ave, Croydon

DISTANCE
18.5km one-way

DURATION
3–5 hours return

 Ringwood train station

The thought of another creek trail may have you rolling your eyes, but this one's a must for nature-lovers. Starting at the scenic confluence of the Yarra River and the Mullum Mullum Creek, it's a ride that heads south-east along Templestowe and Warrandyte's eucalypt-filled reserves. You'll cycle through the suburbs of Doncaster and Donvale then the path briefly links up with the East Link Trail to wind through Melbourne's outer east. Riding on through Mitcham and Ringwood, you'll follow the creek trail, which passes by Eastland Shopping Centre before finishing up in Croydon.

Anniversary (Outer Circle) Trail

START
Earl St, Kew East

DISTANCE
16km one-way

FINISH
Hughesdale station,
Murrumbeena

DURATION
3-4 hours return

East Camberwell, Willison, Hartwell, Burwood,
Alamein train stations

Linking up with the Main Yarra Trail is this jaunt along the old Outer
Circle train line that ran through Melbourne's south-east suburbs
from 1890 to 1926. Kicking off from the meeting point of the Eastern
Fwy and Chandler Hwy, it's a route where 19th-century steam trains
would chug through the leafy suburbs of Kew, Deepdene, Canterbury,
Camberwell, Glen Iris and Ashburton. It makes for a leisurely few hours'
ride as you make your way along a path that mixes parkland with trail-
side cafes. Just beyond Alamein station, the bike path meets up with
the Gardiners Creek Trail before continuing further south just a short
ride from Chadstone Shopping Centre, which, despite its name, isn't
in the suburb of Chadstone, but Malvern East. At Hughesdale station
the trail then merges into the Djerring Trail to set you on a whole
new adventure.

Eastern Dandenong Ranges Trail

 START
Clematis station

FINISH
Gembrook station

 DISTANCE
14km one-way

DURATION
4–6 hours return

Belgrave train station

So you've done the ride out to Puffing Billy along the **Belgrave Rail Trail** (p94) but are still wanting to check out more of the Dandenong Ranges? Well, lucky for you, this undulating outer-city bush trail leads you further into the area's lush forested interior as you pass by a series of quaint townships. Starting out from Puffing Billy's Clematis station (train travel only by special ticket), the gravel trail runs alongside the tracks of the historic scenic railway to zip you through some wonderful natural scenes of towering tree ferns, bushland and rolling farmland as you pass by the towns of Emerald and Cockatoo before finishing up at Gembrook station. Given you've come this far, why not combine your ride with a trip on the iconic steam train itself? In which case you can disembark at Lakeside station to hire a bike from Cog (`cogbikesaustralia.com.au/cog-bikes-lakeside-hire`) from where you'll pedal on for the remainder of the ride. Fun for the entire family, guaranteed!

Acknowledgements

Firstly, we'd like to say a huge thanks to the entire team at Hardie Grant for putting this book together. This includes Melissa Kayser for giving us the opportunity to work on it and for guiding the project, and Amanda Louey for steering the ship in her calm and thoughtful manner, with plenty of laughs along the way. We'd like to extend a big thank you to our wonderful editor, Susan Keogh, one of the best in the business, who worked tirelessly on this. Also thank you to the very talented illustrator and cartographer, Alex Hotchin, whose beautiful work really brought the book to life. Finally, thank you to all the kind folk who generously gave their time to let us pick their brains for the interviews – Max Bohac, Tony Cavallaro, Fam Charko, Tahnee Edwards, Dave Graney, Ann McGregor, Belinda McKenzie, Kendrah Morgan, Nathan Muller, Daisy Smith, Lou Storti, Stuart Tripp and Jayne Tuttle.